The Bettine,
Lady Abingdon
Collection

The Bettine, Lady Abingdon Collection

THE BEQUEST OF MRS T.R.P. HOLE

A Handbook

Sarah Medlam

VICTORIA AND ALBERT MUSEUM

First published by the
Victoria and Albert Museum
London, 1996

The Victoria and Albert Museum
London SW7 2RL

© The Board of Trustees of the
Victoria and Albert Museum 1996

Sarah Medlam asserts her moral right to be
identified as author of this book

ISBN: 1 85177 179 4

A catalogue record for this book is available
from the British Library

Designed by Area
Printed in Italy

Contents

ACKNOWLEDGEMENTS

6

This handbook has involved the work of many people, both in the Museum and outside it. Our first and greatest thanks go to the late Mrs T.R.P. Hole, whose generosity brought this collection to the Museum. The project for a commemorative handbook of the Bettine, Lady Abingdon Collection was initiated by Simon Jervis of the Furniture & Woodwork Collection. His elevation to the Directorship of the Fitzwilliam Museum meant that his own plan to write such a book had to be shelved. His successor as Curator in the Collection of Furniture & Woodwork, Christopher Wilk, was determined that the project should go ahead and the Museum supported him. He has followed the project closely and his suggestions have consistently improved my text. Mrs Hole's executors have kept in regular contact with the project, and Mr Clapson kindly read the drafts of certain sections of the book. Several colleagues worked with Simon Jervis at the time of the Bequest, and in particular Richard Edgcumbe, John Mallet, John Murdoch and Anna Somers Cocks were involved in choosing items which were to come to the Museum.

In preparing this handbook I am grateful for the help of many colleagues in the Collections, in the National Art Library, and in other sections of the Museum, amongst whom I would specially like to thank Michael Archer, Geoffrey Barlow, Lesley Burton, Mary Butler, John Coast, Katherine Coombs, Lucy Cullen, Jo Darrah, Avril Hart, Timothy Hayes, Wendy Hefford, Robin Hildyard, John Kitchin, Karen Livingstone, Gwyn Miles, Elizabeth Miller, Ronald Parkinson, David Pearson, Eoin Shalloo, Timothy Stevens, Rosamund Sykes, Emma Taylor, Moira Thunder, Madeleine Tilley, Marjorie Trusted, Gillian Varley and Rowan Watson. Particular thanks are due to my colleagues in the Metalwork, Silver and Jewellery Collection, Anthony North, Clare Phillips, Sally Dormer and Louise Hofman, who undertook the careful checking of marks, research and writing of the entries for the jewellery and silver and the organization of necessary photography. They were much helped by the efforts of Catherine Arminjon, Michèle Bilimoff, M. Haas and Evelyne Possémé in Paris; T.M.J. Davidson, Teresa Buxton and Madame Jais of Cartier; Daniel Reveyron and Thierry Robert of Boucheron; Diana Scarisbrick and the staff of Chaumet, Paris; and David Beasley of Goldsmiths'

Hall, London. Gareth Williams, in particular, deserves my thanks for his practical help in scheduling the photography of the furniture. Clare Vandermeersch, as a student intern, worked on the early stages of the project. Photographs were patiently taken by several members of the V&A Photographic Studio. In particular I would like to thank Philip Barnard who undertook the photography of all the furniture and Dominic Naish who photographed the metalwork and jewellery. With James Yorke I discussed matters relating to Lord Stuart de Rothesay's collecting, and he provided me with useful references from his personal files. Clive Wainwright had already done work on Highcliffe for his book, *The Romantic Interior*. I am grateful to him for a number of suggestions of sources and for reading the essay on Lord Stuart de Rothesay's purchasing.

For information about Lord and Lady Abingdon and Mr and Mrs Hole I am indebted to Mrs Hole's sister, Mrs Norma Hacket and to her nephew and his wife, Mr and Mrs Neil Hacket. Information was also sent to me by her cousin, Miss Helen Thornton. Friends of Mrs Hole also provided help, in particular Mrs Caverhill, Mrs Rosemary Daniell, Mr Etherington-Smith, Sister Columba O'Neill and Mrs Joyce Wareham. Mr Nigel Percy-Davis kindly provided the photograph of The Oak House.

For permission to visit various properties and inspect furniture my thanks are due to the Marquess of Northampton, to Sir Christopher Mallaby, HM Ambassador to France and to Christchurch Borough Council. The visits were made easy and pleasant by the efforts of James Alabaster of Christie's, Elizabeth Bourgey-Loyer and Christine Warren of the British Embassy, Paris, Alan McAinsh of Castle Ashby and Judith Plumley and Ashley Harman of Christchurch Borough Council. For help with various bouts of library and archive work and for permission to reproduce the documents quoted I would like to thank the governing bodies and the staffs of the Archives Nationales, Paris, BBC Written Archives Centre, the British Library, Christchurch Borough Library, Country Life Picture Library, the Imperial War Museum, the National Library of Scotland, the National Monuments Record, The Red House Museum, Christchurch, the library of the FCO Overseas Property Division, the Archive of the National Portrait Gallery and the County Record Offices of Dorset, Northamptonshire and Staffordshire. To the Duke of Buccleuch I am grateful for permission to quote from his family papers. Colleagues and friends outside the Museum who helped with information or opinion included Simon Jervis in Cambridge; Ian Gow and Margaret Swain in Edinburgh; John Cornforth, Joseph Friedman and John Hardy in London; Martin Chapman in Los Angeles; Marie-Noëlle de Grandry, Ulrich Leben, Christophe Leribault, Côme Remy and Jean-Pierre Samoyault in Paris; Christian Baulez and Denise Ledoux-Lebas at Versailles. Many unkown to me helped through their writings, listed in the bibliography, and I was particularly fortunate to be able to draw on recent biographies of Lord Stuart de Rothesay (by Robert Franklin) and Maréchal Ney (by Eric Perrin).

But above all I would like to express my gratitude to my colleagues in the Furniture & Woodwork Collection for supporting me in this project during a year in which many others clamoured for attention. Permission to reproduce illustrations was kindly given by those listed below. All other illustrations are reproduced by permission of the Trustees of the Victoria & Albert Museum.

Aerofilms Limited: fig. 10

BBC Photograph Library and Archive: fig. 4

Country Life Picture Library: figs 13-19

Mrs R Daniel: fig. 7

Mr N Percy-Davis: fig. 6

Royal Commission on Historical Monuments: fig. 12

Dr Clive Wainwright: fig. 11

Westminster Press: fig. 2

8

Fig. 1
Elizabeth, Countess of
Abingdon and Lindsey
(1896-1978), about 1935,
wearing a double-clip
brooch which forms part
of the Bequest (M.33)

PREFACE

In June 1986 the Museum received an unexpected letter offering a bequest of Empire furnishings. The letter was written on behalf of Mrs T.R.P. Hole of Iwerne Minster in Dorset. Over the next few months, while Mrs Hole battled with illness, several colleagues worked with her in choosing items which might come to the Museum and in making dispositions which were to guarantee that her bequest was not only to be one of the largest that has come to the Museum in recent years, but also one which came, most generously, without restraints or conditions.

The generosity and the care with which Mrs Hole sought to ensure that the bequest would bring maximum benefit to the Museum is all the more remarkable in view of the fact that she considered herself to be acting only as a trustee. It was made clear from the start that she wished the bequest to be known as 'The Bettine, Lady Abingdon Collection'.

In 1978 the Countess of Abingdon had left to her close friends, Mr and Mrs Hole, the remaining furniture, pictures and other works of art from the collections of Highcliffe Castle, Dorset, built in the 1830s by her kinsman Lord Stuart de Rothesay. The Earl and Countess of Abingdon (figs 1 and 2) had been lifelong friends of Mr and Mrs Hole.

Items were chosen for several Museum collections, in most cases inheritances from the estate of Lord Stuart de Rothesay. However, the Metalwork, Silver & Jewellery Collection was also pleased to strengthen very substantially its holdings of 20th-century jewellery through the acquisition of a large group of pieces that had been the personal property of Lady Abingdon.

Additionally, the V&A became the residuary legatee of Mrs Hole's estate, including the funds that had come from Lady Abingdon, augmented by the posthumous sale of Mrs Hole's house and of certain items from the Collection, as agreed in discussions with her. Her generosity brought to the Museum over £800,000, one of the largest bequests the Museum has ever received.

Such bequests provide valuable trust funds which allow the Museum to continue its programmes of gallery improvements, new building, conservation and research, to support all facets of Museum work and not only that of acquisition. A forthcoming major project is the re-display of the galleries of British Art and Design. With present restraints on

9

Fig. 2
The 8th Earl of Abingdon and 13th Earl of Lindsey (1887-1963), about 1950, shown in the London flat with several pieces from the Highcliffe collections

government funding the Museum must raise monies from outside sources for all such projects. Frequently such funding is dependent on the Museum finding matching funds from its own resources. It is only by the generosity of benefactions such as this that new developments become possible.

It had been the quite natural wish of Mrs Hole that the Collection should be kept together, but she quickly understood the difficulties of giving such promises in perpetuity. In fact a representative selection of the furniture was immediately displayed in the galleries then being created to show the arts of Europe and America in the 19th century (Galleries 8 and 9). Almost all the ceramics are shown in the Materials and Techniques galleries of the Ceramics Collection (Galleries 128 and 129), the jewellery (which was shown as a complete collection in the year following the Bequest) is well-represented in the Jewellery galleries (Galleries 91-3) and the gilt-bronzes prompted a temporary exhibition on the subject, which showed some of the pieces from this Collection with others already in the V&A. The Museum also undertook to record the Bettine, Lady Abingdon Collection permanently by publishing a handbook. We are very pleased now to redeem our pledge and to celebrate a most generous bequest to the Museum.

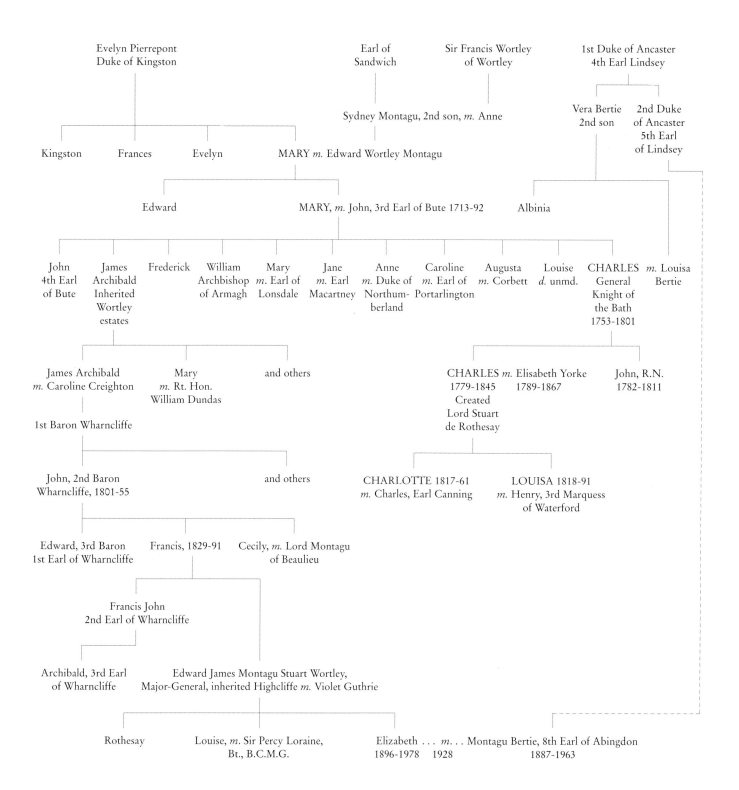

Fig. 3
Family tree of Bettine, Lady Abingdon

The Bettine, Lady Abingdon Collection

Almost all the items in the Bettine, Lady Abingdon Collection, except her personal jewellery, came to her from her kinsman, Charles Stuart (fig. 8), Lord Stuart de Rothesay (1779-1845), who built the Gothic house Highcliffe Castle, Hampshire, which was her home until 1949.

Lord Stuart de Rothesay, a grandson of the 3rd Earl of Bute, was an active and celebrated diplomat throughout his life. His personal passion for building, which led him to become a large-scale purchaser of furniture and pictures, is the subject of the following essay (pp. 19-43). After his death in 1845 the house remained in the family. His two daughters had married respectively Viscount Canning (1812-62) and the Marquess of Waterford (1811-59).[1] Both women were celebrated beauties and accomplished amateur artists. Lady Canning died young, in 1861, while her husband was serving as Governor General of India. After the death of their mother in 1867 Highcliffe Castle passed to her younger sister, Lady Waterford, who held it until her death in 1891. Neither she nor her sister had children and in the very last year of her life she sought diligently for a suitable heir for her Highcliffe property, finally settling it on Edward James Montagu Stuart Wortley, the son of Lord Wharncliffe, her cousin, and a direct descendant of Lord Bute (for the family tree see fig. 3).

General Stuart Wortley's wife, Violet, was a sedulous recorder of family history and investigator of family papers. Her several books on the family prove the starting point for any work on the building of Highcliffe and the formation of its collections.[2] She had been educated in France and Germany as well as Britain and continued the cosmopolitan tradition of Highcliffe.

Their only son, Rothesay, died young in 1927, and the future of the castle became insecure. When, in the following year, their younger daughter, Elizabeth (always known as Bettine; 1894-1978), married the 8th Earl of Abingdon (1887-1963, also the 13th Earl of Lindsey from 1938), he bought the castle for her from her father. During the 1930s the house continued to be used as a centre for lavish entertaining, in addition to the Abingdon's London house. Lady Abingdon moved in circles in which Lord Stuart de Rothesay would have felt at home, and indeed part of her childhood was spent in Paris when her father was serving as Military Attaché to the British Embassy. She was a noted beauty and a woman of fashion, and the beginning of her collection of contemporary jewellery dates from this inter-war period.

During the Second World War she led an active life of travelling to raise funds in America for European refugees under the aegis of a committee called the Refugees of England Inc. She established collection centres in 82 American cities and raised more than £1,000,000. Britons, French, Czechoslovaks, Norwegians, Greeks, Poles and Belgians benefited from her efforts. After the war she received the Légion d'honneur from the French government. She was

12

Fig. 4
Tahu Hole, 1956

accused by the Nazis of spying. Certainly she was involved to some extent in diplomatic action before Italy entered the war in 1940, at a time when her brother-in-law, Sir Percy Loraine, was serving as Ambassador in Rome. During 1941 Lady Abingdon was largely in the United States. On her return to Britain she undertook fundraising for Toc H and finally accepted a liaison role with the Entr'aide Français Pour la Liberation, another refugee organization.

In 1949 it became clear that Highcliffe could no longer be kept up. The house was once more without an heir, and Lord and Lady Abingdon spent much of their time in London. The staff on which such a large house depended had become increasingly difficult to find, and the austerities of post-war Britain did not encourage confidence that such spaces as these could ever again be used as a private house. Plans were made for its disposal and the contents were put up for auction in a three-day sale.[3] From that time Lord and Lady Abingdon lived in a London flat in Curzon Place. The castle was sold to a Roman Catholic missionary order for a seminary.

Highcliffe remained in institutional use for nearly 20 years. By 1967 it was empty again and in that year and the next it suffered two disastrous fires, which brought it to dereliction. Its history at this time was a sorry one, but Christchurch Borough Council has now started a programme of conservation of the buildings and the first stage (the restoration of the conservatory) was completed in 1994, with work on the rest of the house to follow, funded by a grant from the Heritage Lottery Fund.[4]

The friendship between the Abingdons and Mr and Mrs Tahu Hole had been of very long standing. Lady Abingdon and Mrs Hole had been friends since their youth. Tahu Hole (1908-1985; fig. 4) had come to Britain in the late 1930s as a journalist, after working on newspapers in his native New Zealand and in Australia on the *Sydney Morning Herald*. During the war he began working for the BBC, where he continued his career until 1960.[5] In the years immediately after the war Mr and Mrs Hole spent much time at Highcliffe. In the 1940s Tahu Hole wrote the preface to Violet Stuart Wortley's books of family history and reminiscence, *Magic in the Distance* and *Life Without Theory*. He seems to have been fascinated by the Abingdons, and in 1972 when he published a somewhat anecdotal history of the castle and its inhabitants (entitled *Fragments from a Family Tapestry*) he spoke of them as his 'closest companions' and recorded their 'firm friendship for thirty-five years'.[6]

In 1930 in New Zealand he had married Joyce Margaret Wingate (1906-86; fig. 5). She was an Englishwoman, one of three daughters of an officer in the merchant navy, who died when she was a child. Her grandfather had been the Scottish academician Sir James Lawton Wingate (1846-1924), and both Mr and Mrs Hole drew and painted as an amateur interest. Drawings by each of them and etchings by Tahu Hole (who signed 'Ronald Pearce' from his full name

Fig. 5
Miss Joyce Wingate (later Mrs T.R.P. Hole) by Polly Hurry, 1929 (P.5)

Tahu Ronald Pearce Hole) are included in the Bequest. Though there is no evidence that either of them followed a formal programme of training in art, Joyce Hole certainly took lessons in her early life and continued to paint portraits and flower studies in oils up to the year of her death.

After Lord Abingdon's death in 1963 Lady Abingdon lived much of the time with Mr and Mrs Hole until her death in 1978. It was possibly as a result of a family connection of the Abingdons that they decided to move from London to Iwerne Minster, Dorset (Lord Abingdon's great uncle, the 2nd Lord Wolverton (1824-87), had built Iwerne Minster House – now a school – in 1878, using the architect Alfred Waterhouse). The relative closeness of the site of Highcliffe may also have influenced their choice. In Iwerne Minster Mr and Mrs Hole bought The Oak House, built in 1921 (fig. 6) to the designs of M. H. Baillie Scott (1865-1945) as a village hall and community centre, at the expense of Mr Ismay, who had acquired the estate from the family of Lord Wolverton. This large, half-timbered building appeared considerably older, though its architectural style was somewhat at odds with the traditional stone buildings of Dorset. By the time that it was acquired by the Holes it had assumed the appearance and garden of a comfortable early 20th-century country house, the original double-height main hall, where village dances and film shows had been held, becoming a large drawing-room.

In 1979 Mr and Mrs Hole were able in their turn to offer the village a new hall when they undertook the purchase and restoration of the charming, plain, stone building of the Ebenezer chapel (1810) as the Abingdon Memorial Hall.

Having no close relatives, Lady Abingdon left all her possessions to Mr and Mrs Hole on her death in 1978. After Tahu Hole died in November 1985 it became the mission of Joyce Hole (fig. 7) to find a suitable home for the Collection, one which would honour its importance.

14   The attention of the Museum was first drawn to the Empire furniture, from a period which was poorly represented in the V&A's own collections in 1987, when plans were in hand for a new gallery of 19th-century decorative arts from the European mainland and North America. Particularly welcome were the pieces from the collection of Maréchal Ney. Additionally, the Bettine, Lady Abingdon Collection included furnishing bronzes (fenders, candelabra, candlesticks) which had been bought at the same time as the furniture. Smaller items, which were certainly bought by Lord and Lady Stuart de Rothesay, included candlesticks and jewellery stands and other little trinkets in mother-of-pearl and gilt-bronze (the so-called Palais Royal wares) and ceramics. The Silver, Metalwork & Jewellery Collection was particularly enriched by a number of snuff boxes and a 19th-century presentation box with an inscription from the Corporation of Abingdon to the then Earl of Abingdon. The choice of pieces for the Prints, Drawings & Paintings Collection was more varied, and included paintings collected by Lord Stuart de Rothesay, a small group of family miniatures and a large collection of the drawings of Lord Stuart de Rothesay's two daughters, Lady Canning and Lady Waterford. These, with other pieces chosen for the Collections of Sculpture and of Textiles & Dress, both document the large collections of Highcliffe (now dispersed) or individually extend the scope

Fig. 6
The Oak House, Iwerne Minster

of the Museum's collections. For the National Art Library a group of books was chosen both as desirable additions to the Special Collections of the Library and as representative of Lord Stuart de Rothesay's own large and important collection of books.[7] A high proportion of them carry one of five versions of the Stuart arms on their bindings.

Lady Abingdon's collection was not solely of the pieces she had inherited from her kinsman. The Museum was also extremely pleased to be offered her personal collection of jewellery. This included some earlier pieces which may have come by family descent but is essentially a collection of contemporary jewels bought by and for Lady Abingdon from Cartier, Boucheron and other important makers. Such pieces were thinly represented in the Museum's collection and to acquire such a varied collection, many of which can be fully-documented, is a rare opportunity.

Fig. 7
Mrs Hole, 1986,
in the year before her death

NOTES FOR PAGES 11-15

1. Augustus Hare, *The Story of Two Noble Lives*, 1893.
2. Violet Stuart Wortley's books include *Highcliffe and the Stuarts*, 1927, and *Magic in the Distance*, 1949, both of which drew extensively on the family papers before their dispersal.

3. Christie's, at Highcliffe Castle, 5-7 June 1949. I am grateful to Mrs Joyce Wareham for lending me the copy with Lord Abingdon's annotations.
4. Giles Worsley, 'Highcliffe Castle, Dorset', *Country Life*, CLXXIX (1986), pp.1428-32. Nina James Gibbs discussed the full range of options for the future of the castle in *Highcliffe Castle: A need for*

Action (unpublished thesis submitted 1987 for BA in Art History at Richmond College).
5. Leonard Miall, *Inside the BBC*, 1994, pp.123-33.
6. Tahu Hole, *Fragments from a Family Tapestry*, 1972.
7. See pp.25-6, 95-9.

Chronology of
Lord Stuart de Rothesay's Life

1779	Charles Stuart born 2 January, eldest son of Major General the Hon. Sir Charles Stuart, KB
1797	Matriculates at Christ Church, Oxford, but leaves after one year
1801	Appointed as Secretary to the Legation at Vienna, he travels to Berlin, Warsaw and St Petersburg before taking up his appointment
1802	Peace of Amiens
1804	Secretary to the Embassy at St Petersburg
1806-7	Ambassador in St Petersburg
1807	Present at the signing of the Treaty of Tilsit, 25 June
1808	Returns on leave to England and re-purchases part of the Highcliffe estate
1808-9	Special mission to Spain as joint *chargé d'affaires*
1809	Special mission to Austria
1810-14	Envoy Extraordinary and Minister Plenipotentiary in Lisbon. Created Count of Machico, Marquis of Angra and Knight Grand Cross of the Order of the Tower and the Sword
1812	Invested with the insignia of Civil Knight Grand Cross of the Order of the Bath and made a Privy Councillor
1814	Envoy Extraordinary and Minister Plenipotentiary (*ad interim*) in Paris from 11 June
1815	Minister Plenipotentiary at The Hague
1815-24	Ambassador Extraordinary and Plenipotentiary in Paris

1816	Marriage to Lady Elizabeth Yorke, in February
1817	Birth of their daughter, Charlotte
1818	Birth of a second daughter, Louisa
1824	Death of Louis XVIII; Stuart recalled to London
1825-6	Ambassador on special mission to Portugal and Brazil
1828	Wellington becomes Prime Minister. Stuart is raised to a barony as Lord Stuart de Rothesay of the Isle of Bute
1828-31	Ambassador Extraordinary and Plenipotentiary in Paris for a second term
1830	Revolution in France. Charles X and his family go into exile in Britain. Louis Philippe becomes King of the French
1831	In January Stuart is recalled, though he does not return to London immediately
1835	Marriage of his daughter Charlotte to Charles Canning, later Viscount Canning
1841-4	Ambassador to Russia
1842	Marriage of his daughter Louisa to the Marquess of Waterford
1844	Ill-health forces his resignation and return to Britain
1845	Death of Lord Stuart de Rothesay, 6 November
1861	Death of Charlotte, Lady Canning
1867	Death of Lady Stuart de Rothesay
1891	Death of Louisa, Lady Waterford

Lord Stuart de Rothesay, his Purchasing and Building

Charles Stuart (1779-1845; fig. 8) is best known for his powerful and active diplomatic career during which, from 1801-44, he served in Austria, Russia, Spain, The Netherlands, France, Portugal and Brazil, acting often as special envoy and several times returning to one or other of the embassies as he rose through the ranks from secretary to ambassador. For many of his serving years he managed to keep himself at the centre of the action on the European stage, during times of exceptional political and diplomatic upheaval.[8] In 1805, when in Vienna, he helped the imperial family to flee, and in 1807 he was serving with the embassy at St Petersburg at the time of Tilsit.[9] He seems to have moved about Europe much as other people move about a single city, and his natural aptitude for languages must have served as the key to this ability to feel at home as much in Lisbon or Vienna as in Paris, and perhaps more so in those cities than in London.

All the time that his public life was taken up with the diplomacy of the Napoleonic wars and their aftermath, Charles Stuart was filling his private time with plans for the great house which he was to build at Highcliffe, near Christchurch, Hampshire (now Dorset) in the 1830s, on land which had belonged to his grandfather, and which he bought back over several years with a careful persistence. He was a grandson of the 18th-century Prime Minister, the 3rd Earl of Bute (1713-92). Though born a commoner, Charles Stuart was made a Knight of the Bath in 1812 and in 1828 was created Baron Stuart de Rothesay, taking his title from the family seat on the Scottish island of Bute.

The Highcliffe estate had come into the Stuart family in the late 1760s when it was purchased by the 3rd Earl of Bute, who had admired the setting overlooking Christchurch Bay and the Isle of Wight during a botanical expedition. The first family house was built in 1773 (fig. 9) to the design of Robert Adam, who was to work for Lord Bute at Luton, Kenwood and Lansdowne House. It included a laboratory and conservatory to cater to his botanical interests and carefully planted grounds.[10] However, for all his interest in natural history, he had chosen a poor site, one naturally prone to subsidence as the sea worked relentlessly at the coastline. By the time his son inherited in 1792, the house was severely unstable and by 1798 it was demolished and the land sold. His grandson must have known the house in childhood and clearly held it in romantic veneration as his family seat.

The young Charles Stuart's determination to build another house on the site is recorded from at least 1807 in letters to his mother, although it was not until the 1830s that the new Highcliffe was built, a theatrically Gothic house in the tradition, if not to the scale, of Fonthill. In the course of a brief visit to England in 1808 Charles Stuart set in train the re-purchase of part of the orginal Highcliffe estate, sold by his father. A smaller house had been

erected by the intermediate owner but this was clearly not going to be enough. He left his mother in charge. From her house at Bure Homage nearby she superintended some of the farming and business matters on the estate, and in 1808 he was encouraging her to order the making and stockpiling of bricks, presumably with the idea of building in mind: 'if I bake all Bure Common into bricks so much the better; I will use what I want and sell the rest'.[11]

But Charles Stuart was only partially minded to build his house and settle down. In the period 1810-15 he was not only caught up in important and thrilling events on the Continent, but was at the same time leading a sociable bachelor life. He found, like many Englishmen of the period, that France was a heady delight, and clearly he liked the sense of being at the hub of the universe. On 1 May 1814, again in a letter to his mother, he described life in Paris:

> The town is very entertaining from the variety of Ambassadors and Envoys, and other important people. We lead the most agreeable life. I dine tomorrow at Malmaison. Prince Eugène and the Queen of Holland will both be there. I like Josephine better than anyone I have seen here, and think all her family delightful! Hortense especially so; however I do not mention this, as I should be in *mauvais odeur* with the new Court![12]

At this time he was charged by the Duke of Wellington with finding a house to serve as a British Embassy. He looked at several *hôtels particuliers*, including the Elysée Bourbon which had belonged to Caroline Murat (and was soon to be occupied by the Emperor of Russia) and the hôtels de Noailles and de Cambacérès; but Wellington finally settled on the Hôtel Charôst, which had been given by Napoleon to his sister Pauline Borghese in 1803 and which had the decided advantage of retaining most of its furnishings. Pauline, anxious not to be outdone by the establishments of her siblings Joseph and Caroline, had furnished the *hôtel* in the most luxurious and fashionable manner, employing the architect Pierre-François-Léonard Fontaine (1762-1853) and using some furniture that she already owned (from her first husband's house, the Château de Montgobert) as well as new giltwood mirrors, pier tables and suites of giltwood seat furniture provided by the most fashionable of the Empire cabinet makers, with the very conscious purpose of proclaiming the political power of the Bonaparte family.[13] The inventory taken in 1804 unfortunately does not survive but that taken in 1814 on the sale of the house to the British government records the sumptuous wall-hangings of silk in strong colours, the extensive suites of giltwood furniture and the quantities of gilt-bronze

Fig. 9
Highcliffe, the earlier house designed by Adam; transfer print by Stone, Coquerel and Legros on a soup plate made at Creil and Montereau, about 1815 (C.12)

20

candelabra, chandeliers and fireplace furniture which gave the rooms such a dazzling appearance.[14] For Pauline it had been a house for entertaining and it was just such a house that was needed for the British Embassy.

Charles Stuart was clearly a good man to entrust with such a purchase, an incipient collector himself and a would-be builder, as well as a highly sociable man. He moved in the wide circle of francophile English who were about to launch into the new enthusiasm of collecting and to make Britain in the 19th century the richest depository of French furniture and the decorative arts of the 17th and 18th centuries. The travelling for pleasure of the British, which re-started during the Peace of Amiens in 1802, came to an abrupt end with political imprisonment for many, but immediately travelling became possible again they returned to Paris both as tourists and as residents.[15]

In 1815, while serving in a short-lived post as Minister Plenipotentiary at The Hague during the Hundred Days, Sir Charles Stuart was corresponding with Lady Elizabeth Yorke (1789-1867), youngest daughter of Philip, 3rd Earl of Hardwicke (1757-1834).[16] It is likely that he had first met her in England or in Paris in the previous year, and the matter of a marriage between them seems to have been arranged by his friends the Misses Berry, who understood the value of this plain woman in her late twenties.[17] Stuart was not entirely pleased to settle into married life but Lady Elizabeth's upbringing made her an ideal wife for an ambassador, and her large dowry was no mean inducement to a man who already had ambitions to build. They were married in February 1816, after Sir Charles had been confirmed as Ambassador in Paris, and moved into the Hôtel Charôst for a brilliant ambassadorial reign.

The Stuarts occupied the Hôtel Charôst from 1816-24 and for a second term from 1828-31. During these periods and in the interregnum (when Lord and Lady Granville were appointed after the death of Louis XVIII), various alterations were undertaken but in essence, throughout the reigns of Louis XVIII and Charles X, the Empire interiors remained little changed. Sir Charles and Lady Stuart were very much at home in Paris society of the 1820s and gave lavish entertainments, spending on these much of their private income. When the Granvilles succeeded the Stuarts for a second time at the Embassy in the 1831, Lady Granville complained of the parsimony of the government which restricted her funds for lighting the rooms as Lady Stuart had done.[18] Lady Stuart was highly popular with the re-established Bourbons and a particular friend was the Duchesse de Berry with whom the Stuarts shared the new enthusiasm for the Gothic, known in France as the *style troubadour*. Combining the two enthusiasms, for historicism and for entertainment, the Stuarts were closely involved in arrangements for the splendid fancy-dress ball on 2 March 1829 at the Tuileries. The Duchesse de Berry took the role of Mary Stuart, with Lady Stuart as Marie de Lorraine and her daughter, Louisa, as one of her attendants.[19] In the same year the Stuarts gave their own *bal costumé* to celebrate the birthday of George IV, a glowing occasion described by Lady Morgan.[20] Thus while living amongst the sternest classicism of the Empire, the Stuarts were already flirting with a romantic medievalism, as if in training for the juxtaposition of styles which was to characterize Highcliffe.

Charles Stuart's English friends were from a circle where collecting was a major obsession. He was a contemporary of Lord Yarmouth, later the 3rd Marquess of Hertford (1777-1842), the great collector, with whom he spent much time in Paris. He knew Lord Lowther, later Earl of Lonsdale (1787-1872), and through him had contact with the Prince Regent and with the Marchioness of Conyngham (d.1861), all of whom were active collectors of French furniture and the decorative arts in the years following the peace. A letter filed with those of 1832 in the Stuart de Rothesay correspondence in the National Library of Scotland, but with a date which should clearly be read as 1822, from Brighton and signed Francis Conyngham, records that the Prince 'expects shortly several small articles from Paris which he has ordered should be sent to your office & wishes that they may be forwarded straight to His majesty by your Bag.'[21] The guest list of the Embassy in the years immediately following 1815 included the names of many English aristocrats who were to establish themselves sometimes for months or years at a time in Paris and who were to buy French furnishings for their houses in Britain.[22] Already in 1814 the Duke and Duchess of Rutland were at the Embassy and later the Earl and Countess of Mansfield were regular visitors, Lady Mansfield standing proxy for Queen Charlotte as godmother at the christening of Stuart's daughter in 1817. A letter of 7 September 1816 to Sir Charles Stuart concerns the formation of the Cercle Français, where members included many of the collecting coterie.[23] As Violet Stuart Wortley later wrote:

> [He] could exercise his knowledge of art in finding bibelots for Lady Jersey
> and his love of books in pursuing rare ones on behalf of Lord Spencer. One
> of his favourite recreations was attending the auction rooms with Lord
> Hertford.[24]

Surrounded as they were by 'collecting' Englishmen and with Sir Charles's thoughts already on the dream of re-creating Highcliffe, it is understandable that he should drift into the habit of buying. His first purchases may have been to supplement the furnishings of the Embassy, both utilitarian and decorative. It has been suggested that he may have acquired for the Embassy the impressive Thomire *surtout de table* which cannot be traced in the 1814 inventory.[25] Certainly he seems to have begun his own purchasing with the acquisition of almost contemporary Empire furniture for immediate use. The undersides of several of the pieces in the Bequest carry paper labels with the arms of Sir Charles Stuart, inscribed with his name, and a second heart-shaped label with the date 20 August 1816. Many of the pieces of Pauline Borghese's furniture which survive in the British Embassy today carry labels of a similar shape, relating to the 1814 inventory.[26] The presence of the similarly shaped labels with the later date makes it tempting to connect these pieces also with Pauline Borghese. One set of chairs (F.13) may relate to a description in her inventory of chairs which were no longer in the Embassy by 1841, but the identification is not absolute and the problem of the discrepancy in dates remains. A possible explanation is that Sir Charles Stuart, wishing two years later to make an inventory of the furniture which he was beginning to buy on his own account, employed the broker Michelot who had drawn up the 1814 inventory, and that the labels are his speciality.[27] Certainly the market for the selling of such pieces was understood in Paris. On 30 November 1814 Michelot wrote to Pauline Borghese about the possiblility of selling her jewel cabinet which had been made by Jacob-Desmalter: 'On espère toujours le vendre à quelque anglais, ainsi que votre service de vermeil' ['there is always the hope of selling it to some Englishman, and your silver-gilt service as well'].[28] Stuart was not immune to the buying of furniture for 'souvenir' interest. The seat furniture (F.5, F.6, F.7) by Jacob-Desmalter bears labels indicating its provenance from the collection of Maréchal Ney and the variety of imperial provenances quoted in the 1949 sale catalogue of the contents of Highcliffe suggests that the associations were jealously guarded by the family, although most of them may now be unproveable and some may well have been hopeful. For Sir Charles Stuart it seems likely that both the furniture itself and the personalities with which it was connected retained strong connotations of both elegance and glamour.

The buying of contemporary French furnishings had been established as a particular British taste in the middle of the 18th century when travellers such as the Marquess of Lorne (later 5th Duke of Argyll) and his wife were in Paris (painted there by Drouais in 1763), the Duke and Duchess of Richmond and the Earl of Coventry.[29] There was also a flourishing market for smaller pieces and Horace Walpole's offer to buy Sèvres for his friend Chute in 1765/6 is only the best known example of this taste.[30] The purchases of the famous sets of Boucher/Nielson tapestries for Croome Court, Weston Hall, Moor Park etc. are evidence of a French market firmly aimed at English patrons.[31] Chippendale's little spot of bother over trying to evade customs dues when importing a consignment of 60 French chairs in 1769 is well-known, [32] and was only one incident of a trade which caused the cabinet-makers of London to protest in 1772 and 1773.[33] Protests were, however, in vain and the acceptance of Paris as the fashion leader in furnishings was reinforced with the Prince of Wales' widespread use of French craftsmen in the work on Carlton House in the 1780s.[34] The influence of these schemes is scarcely to be underestimated, both on major works such as the re-fitting of Inveraray by the 5th Duke of Argyll after 1783 and on smaller schemes which involved less direct contact with French craftsmen.[35] Shopping scarcely stopped for the Napoleonic wars. The 7th Earl of Elgin was caught in Paris on his way back from diplomatic duties in Constantinople when the Peace of Amiens broke down. He spent the three years of his imprisonment in commissioning a French architect to design alterations for his house at Broomhall in Fife.[36] In 1804 he purchased furniture in the newest taste from the *marchand-mercier*, Martin-Eloy Lignereux (1750 or 1752-1809), made by the cabinet-maker Adam Weisweiler (1744-1820).[37] At the same time he was acquiring designs for furniture and mounts which it is presumed he intended to use on furniture in the French style to be made in Scotland. In 1815 he was back again in Paris as soon as peace made this possible and was seeking garden designs for Broomhall from Napoleon's own landscape architect, Louis Martin Berthault (1771-1823).[38] The list of English aristocrats who passed through Paris in the period 1815-20 is long, including Alexander Archibald Douglas, Marquess Douglas and his wife (daughter of the collector William Beckford), who succeeded in 1819 as Duke and Duchess of Hamilton; the Duke and Duchess of Newcastle; Lady Holland; Lady Bessborough; Lady Jersey; and Lord and Lady Mansfield.[39] The Duchesses of Richmond and of Beaufort were both at the Waterloo Ball and remained in France. Many aristocrats, like Lord Pembroke, were buying furiously. Lady Hardwicke travelling to stay with the young Stuarts in 1817, wrote to her husband: 'In the inn court at Calais we saw Ld. Bedford & Lord Clancarty who

24 had been just four days at Paris & were returning to England. I believe it was to buy furniture for the Hague that he came.'[40]

It was the purchasing by these enthusiasts in the first decades of the 19th century that set in train the fashion for the collecting of furniture and other decorative arts of earlier periods which became an obsession of so many rich and titled British people in the course of the 19th century. In the 18th century such collecting had been confined to a very few connoisseurs, but by the 1830s the trade in 17th and 18th-century items from Paris (whether bought there or through the growing collectors' trade in London) was immense. Throughout the 1820s, as this trade developed, there are letters to Lord Stuart de Rothesay from Lord Pembroke, Lord Jersey and several others on collecting matters.[41]

The fashion continued to be led by the Prince Regent. His acquisitions in the period 1800 to 1820 show how purchasing and commissioning went hand-in-hand with the beginnings of 'collecting'.[42] Thus a pair of the most severely Empire pedestals veneered in amboyna and mounted with gilt-bronzes, derived from designs by Percier and Fontaine, were received in 1813 (at the height of hostilities, it should be noted). They were placed in the Bow Room at Carlton House. In the same year Robert Fogg, a London dealer who also sold to the other noted and influential collectors William Beckford and the Duke of Northumberland, supplied to Carlton House 'Two Large Cabinets mounted in Or Molou with white Marble tops' which are tentatively identified with two late 17th or early 18th-century cabinets of boulle marquetry.[43] Six years later the Prince was having copies made for use at Brighton of a pier table in the Chinese taste made in the Paris workshop of Adam Weisweiler nearly 30 years before.[44] After his succession in 1820 George IV continued as an avid collector, concentrating more particularly in this decade on the furniture and porcelain of the 18th century.[45] The idea of collecting as the polite accomplishment of a gentleman had begun to develop, and with it an English passion for decorating houses in the styles of the monarchs of the *ancien régime*.[46]

Parallel with the growth of a taste for French arts of the 17th and 18th centuries, a collecting mania also developed in Britain which centred on the recently defeated hero Napoleon. In 1815 Walter Scott was in Paris, with an eye on the events of the day. His admiration for Napoleon resulted more than a decade later in the publication of his *Life* in 1827. He was not the only admirer, and collections of Napoleonic relics were not uncommon. William Beckford and Sir Samuel Rush Meyrick both included Napoleonic material amongst their larger antiquarian collections and one enthusiast, John Sainsbury, devoted all his energies to this topic.[47] Alexander Hamilton, Marquess of Douglas (later Duke of Hamilton), had commissioned a portrait of the Emperor by Jacques-Louis David as early as 1811, was left a *nécessaire de voyage* by Pauline Borghese in 1825 and later acquired further items with Napoleonic interest, including the silver-gilt service of the Emperor.[48] In Britain Napoleon had attained the status of hero as well as national enemy.

Though we know that Sir Charles Stuart was beginning to buy furniture and pictures from the time of his marriage, it was not until the late 1820s that significant records of his architectural and decorating aspirations were recorded in his papers. These papers are understandably extensive, and are now scattered in several deposits.[49] By far the greatest part is related to his diplomatic activities, and there is relatively little that records his purchases and his plans for his houses.

Of all Stuart's interests his book collecting, which was clearly a personal passion, is the best recorded and covers the largest span of years. If we look at the plan of Highcliffe as built (fig. 12), the library, in the south-west corner of the house, was fully as large as the drawing-room and dining-room and was fitted closely with bookcases. It is likely that there was also a library in his London house at 4 Carlton House Terrace. Stuart may have been paying tribute to his grandfather in this interest: Lord Bute was a noted collector of books and had employed the British Resident in Venice to buy for him. But Stuart's interest was also a fashionable one for an educated gentleman of his time. In 1816, almost as soon as he had settled in Paris, Simier Frères were sending information about the details of armorial bindings that he had ordered.[50] Throughout his years in Paris he received and kept information about new editions of classic works and catalogues and information about the sale of collections of books.[51] On 31 July 1817 Crevot, a bookseller in the rue de médicine, was writing to him about accepting a copy of a recently printed map of China as 'amateur et Genereux Protecteur des beaux arts'.[52] Stuart must have relished this kind of flattery, and the booksellers were not lacking in shrewdness in appealing to him in this way. He was sometimes petitioned to recommend books to George IV, also a noted bibliophile.[53] He was certainly seen as a member of a small group of collectors. In 1815 another dealer, Courcelles, was writing to him about deliveries of books for Lord Ashburton and the Duke of Gloucester amongst others: clearly Stuart was acting as a conduit, perhaps to avoid duty or charges of carriage.[54] His correspondence on the matter of book-collecting was not restricted to France: in 1818 he received a letter from Stuttgart about acquiring a catalogue of books published in Germany since 1700.[55] In 1819 a bookseller, Auguste Kraemer, was writing to him from Ratisbon about the sale of the collections of the Prince de Palm, and J. Kraytter of the rue d'Anjou, Paris, was sending him information about different editions of a particular book.[56] A letter from Kraemer on 22 July 1820 lists a number of books and makes clear that Stuart was not merely putting together a reading library but was investing in 16th-century and earlier books, including early literary texts and books of literary history.[57] Cryptic references to purchases of books or offers of books from dealers continue throughout the 1820s and into the 1830s, including payments for agents who were keeping his subscriptions up to date.

In 1822 Stuart published at his own expense the text of an obscure and ancient Portuguese poem. It is possible that this is the work referred to in a letter from E. D. Davenport of Tarporley, Cheshire to Miss Berry in North Audley Street on the subject of Stuart's books.[58] He writes of Stuart being eager to have a correspondent in England from whom he might get 'bibliographical information' and speaks of two editions of the *Cancionere General*, both of the 16th century.[59] Stuart retained a 'bookish' circle of correspondents all his life. There were letters to Henry Ellis, the librarian of the British Museum.[60] In 1833, in a letter to the bibliographer John Martin (1791-1855), Stuart mentions his own two publications: one was a *Catalogue des Livres de la Bibliothèque du Chevalier Stuart Paris. Exprimé à l'Hotel de Son Majesté Brittanique* (1821), and the other (1823, although in the letter Stuart dates it to the

26 previous year) the edition of the early Portuguese poem, *Fragmentos de hum cancioneiro inedito*.[61] Stuart's success in his diplomatic work in Portugal and Brazil was attributed to 'the appreciation he showed for the past achievements of the country and its literature'.[62]

Manuscripts also came to his notice, and in January 1822 he was offered a group relating to English, Scots and Irish history. The letter, stating a price of £600 for the papers, though written in French from an address at 29 rue St Honoré, is signed 'Jno Rock' and may be from an Englishman. He mentions the British government and it is not clear whether he was offering these to Stuart in a personal or ambassadorial capacity.[63] In 1839 a letter from a Mr P. Macpherson, who appears to have been a dealer with whom Lord Stuart de Rothesay had long had dealings, was writing to him from Rome about copies of Jacobite letters which he had examined for Lord Stuart.[64]

After his death Stuart's library was sent to auction in 1855. The sale of the 4323 lots took 15 days and the catalogue well illustrates the ambitious nature of his book collecting.[65]

Clearly Stuart's personal interests were intellectual and artistic, and he was frequently approached with requests to obtain entry for scholars or amateurs to the closed galleries of the Louvre.[66] In 1821 he received a letter from the dealer M. Roger, of the rue de la Jussienne, enclosing the prospectus for an engraving by Corneille Bloemart of the *Holy Family* by Annibale Carracci, from 'le palais des jardins de Montquirinal', by the permission of the Holy Father. The painting was also for sale, described – interestingly for a period when perhaps we imagine that condition was less considered – as 'sur coutil, sans aucun repeint'.[67]

On 27 November 1820 it was Lady Stuart who was was writing about the painting of Jeanne d'Aragon (see P.1):

> We have bought the Jeanne d'Aragon in the old Crawfurd's [Quintin Craufurd's] collection. It is but a copy of the Raffaelle by Giulio Romano, but the original in the Musée having been so much injured, this picture was borrowed to <u>copy</u> from…We have bought only three pictures altogether, though perhaps we may catch one or two more; but we have not trusted ourselves to look at the collection a second time, for fear of getting into the scrape of <u>bargains</u>.[68]

Stuart's first embassy lasted from 1815 to 1824 and though no documentation exists it is likely that the greater part of his purchasing of Empire furniture took place in these years. Much may have been used to supplement the Embassy furnishings. Certainly, on 15 November 1824, Harriet Granville, whose husband was to succeed Stuart, wrote tetchily from Brussels to her sister on the poor state of the Paris Embassy, 'Sir Charles having emptied the rooms to fill innumerable large packing cases, which are all standing about in the ante-rooms and passages'.[69] This might be seen as a charge of appropriating Embassy furniture, but no evidence supports this.

It is also to the end of the first embassy that the earliest acquisitions of architectural salvage for Highcliffe must date. Although Sir Charles Stuart must have been very conscious of his grandfather's Classical house, he himself was veering to the medieval in his dreams for

Fig. 10
Highcliffe Castle from the air, 1951, showing the oriel window from Les Andelys above the main garden door

the new Highcliffe. The major elements that were used in the decoration of his house have been celebrated since it was built.[70] Best known of all were the fragments of the 15th-century Grande Maison at Les Andelys in Normandy, the source of the dramatic oriel window used above the garden entrance (fig. 10). The story has been told and re-told how Stuart saw the demoliton of the house taking place and immediately bought the oriel window and other pieces from the ruins and had them transported to England. Figure 11, first published in 1825 illustrates its destruction.[71] Views of the house by John Sell Cotman had been published only in 1822 in his work with Dawson Turner, *Antiquities of Normandy*.[72] Amongst the drawings of Lady Waterford that came to the Museum in this bequest is a sketchbook (P.58) which includes studies after Cotman's book. Louisa Stuart would have been a small child at time of the demolition of the house, but she may later have encountered this book in her father's library, evidence perhaps of his first interest in the building. Other elements of Highcliffe came from the Abbey of Jumièges which had also been illustrated in *Voyages pittoresques et romantiques dans l'ancienne France – Normandie* with the house from Les Andelys.[73] Other churches undergoing either demolition or 'improvement' provided further elements which are not all identifiable. It is likely that the Jumièges material was removed from the site before October 1824, and the tradition that it was sold to an English 'milord' suggests that it was bought straight away by Stuart, who would have been about to return to London at the end

Fig. 11
Destruction of
La Grande Maison at Les
Andelys
(C. Nodier & J. Taylor,
*Voyages pittoresque et
romantiques dans
l'ancienne France -
Normandy,* 1825)

28 of his first term as ambassador in Paris.[74] Though there is no first-hand record of the date of the purchase, Violet Stuart Wortley stated that Highcliffe was ready for occupation before Stuart set out in March 1825 for his mission to Brazil to arbitrate between Portugal and Brazil in the matter of the independence of the former colony, and suggests that the Les Andelys stone was at least on site at that time.[75] What seems likely is that this 'readiness' was the immediate and modest making-over of the earlier house and that work on the new house did not begin until 1830.[76] Certainly a letter from J.S. Cotman to Lord Stuart de Rothesay, sent from Norwich on 13 July 1828, suggests that the Les Andelys stonework was by then in Stuart's possession. The artist wrote: 'I have no scale or measurement of any kind belonging to the House of Andelys or they must certainly have been sent to you without delay', also thanking Lord Stuart for 'the payment of this amount'.[77] His advice had presumably been sought in the matter of re-erecting the stonework.

In 1828 Stuart was back in Paris, for a second and very welcome reign as ambassador. During this time, he was clearly concerned with ordering in Paris fittings and furniture which would be needed for his new house at Highcliffe and for another in London at 4 Carlton House Terrace. His first interest in a London house was in 1827 and although it was finished by 1831 he seems not to have occupied it himself until 1834. On 28 February 1827 the architect Decimus Burton (1800-81) wrote to him from 8 Regent Street about the plans for the house 'which you purpose to have erected on the Terrace in Carlton House Gardens[sic]', for which three days earlier he had been recommending the products of 'the Marble Works in Esher Street, near Holywell Street, Westminster'.[78] During 1828 and 1829 work continued, as reported in letters to Lord Stuart. On 3 April 1829 a Mr W. Tomline wrote:

> Lord Caledon sent me yesterday a memorial he had drawn up to the
> Treasury for an extension of time and for a communication with Pall Mall.
> He has signed it for you. Your house is totally inaccessible in a carriage.[79]

Two weeks later Mr Tomline was again writing:

> They are beginning to rail off the garden in front of our houses, and from
> the plan it will not be a wide one. I hear you have been giving a most
> splendid entertainment to sixty people, and displayed a very magnificent
> service of Plate.

And on 4 May:

> I am furious and indignant beyond words at the scheme for Nash to build
> stables and let them to us; it is a job solely for Nash to get his five per cent.

for the whole building besides his other Perquisites. Nothing but necessity will prevent my kicking, and nothing but regard for Lowther will prevent my shewing him up if all I hear is true. Nash is everything with the King at this moment, who says he is the only man of business he ever saw that suited him.

But by 29 May he could write:

Your house goes on slowly; the plaster is not yet on the dining-room ceiling.

And when Stuart actually returned to England in 1830 his house was not ready for him, and Lord Hertford offered him the temporary use of Dorchester House.[80] The family occupied the house at No. 4 Carlton House Terrace from 1834 to 1841. Next door, at No. 5, lived Lady Stuart's sister, Catherine, with her husband, the Earl of Caledon.

Little in detail is known about the fittings and furnishings of the house in Carlton House Terrace. Highcliffe seems always to have been Stuart's first interest and in 1841, when Lord Stuart went to St Petersburg, the London house was let to the Prussian Embassy.[81] However, the suave Classicism of the architecture and what little we do know of its interior decoration suggest that the Empire furniture may initially have been intended for this house and may have been transferred subsequently to Highcliffe. Such a differentiation between a town house in the latest fashion and a country house with historical associations would have been common in France at the time.

When Lord Stuart de Rothesay's diplomatic 'reign' in Paris came to an abrupt end after 1830, because his friendship with the previous regime was thought to render him unacceptable to the Orleanist monarchy, he was reluctant to leave Paris and retired, most improperly, to a rented house in Paris while Lord and Lady Granville once again took over the Embassy. The change of ambassadors took place in January 1831 but on 24 December 1830 Lord Palmerston (who was not a friend) had already written, with exquisite diplomacy, to warn Lord Stuart that such breaches of etiquette would not be tolerated:

I know well enough by Experience how agreeable a Residence that Capital always is, & cannot be surprized therefore that People who are not versed in Diplomatic arrangements should assign it to you as your Intended Residence, But a Person so conversant as you are with all the Considerations which bear upon your Branch of the Public Service, would of course be sensible to the Many and obvious Inconveniences which must necessarily arise from the Continued Residence of one ambassador in a Capital where he had recently been succeeded in his public Functions by another.[82]

Despite his wishes, Stuart could not remain indefinitely in Paris.

30　　A handful of letters between Stuart and his agent gives a tantalizing glimpse of the mechanics of shipping what were clearly large quantities of furnishings, architectural fittings and assorted personal possessions. His main agent, as far as we can tell from the occasional letters that survive, was an Englishman who was settled in Paris at 64 rue Amelot, Mr George Gunn. A letter from Mr Gunn dated 7 August provides details of how the material was to be transported. The year seems to read as 1831, though the reference to 'the sudden change in political affairs within the last three days' may suggest 1830, when Charles X abdicated on 6 August. If so, the letter may be interpreted as a precipitate attempt by Stuart to evacuate some of his personal belongings. The letter documents (though does not elucidate) the relationship between Gunn and the London dealer James Nixon, whose label is to be found on one of the chairs (F.9), and mentions introductions which Stuart has provided for Gunn to other possible clients.

My Lord, I duly rec'd yr Lordships both enclosed by Mr Nixon and also yr Lordships letter dated the 1st Inst. – In answer to the first my Lord, I beg to assure yr Lordship that no irregularity shall take place neither at Southampton or Calais but everything forwarded to Mr Nixon – as to the last letter of yr Lordship I beg to say that I duly advised Mr Nixon of Contents of the 31 Cases & since which I have recd a Letter from Mr Nixon informing me of the arrival – but says not a word that he has not received advice from me as to the contents – I am sorry there should be such a want of candour towards me on the part of him and it is not the first time I have had to complain of it even to yr Lordship. Yr Lordship I am sure will do the Justice to say that towards both the Nixons I have always exerted myself in their favour – and I now Cannot account for all the petty back-biting on their part and without cause or reason. I have my Lord hired a Steam boat which is now charging Yr Lordships baggage which will leave Paris on Wednesday Morning and arrive at Havre on Saturday in good time to meet the Vessel and I have apprised Mr Taylor thereof – the whole of the Marble at Labiois[83] will not be finished in time – but no great deal will be left behind – I think my Lord of leaving open in the List 10 Cases – to follow – so as to save paying duties in England = in Case of need – after the arrival of the first part – of the Baggage. I am occupied my Lord in making out a Regular List – but prior to sending one to yr Lordship I shall send my friend Robinson to Havre Wh the steamer & Baggage to verify & add what remain in the Wharehouse of Mr Taylor so as to have everything in order – but yr Lordship shall have a list in due time & Yr Lordships instructions as to Contents strictly adhered to. I have waited upon the Marq. de Coigny & referd by him to Gent. Sebastiani – who has requested me to call again on Tuesday on the Marq. de Coigny which I will not omit attending to & if delivered to me in time shall be packd wh great care.[84]

In respect to the Livries, M. Sottoricolli [possibly a servant] orderd them to be sent to Havre as not in good state enough to be used in London – I propose my <u>Lord Keeping in Paris the Throne & State Livries – in Case</u>, the sudden change which has taken place in political affairs within the <u>last 3 days</u> should <u>call them into Service</u> earlier than was thought of when you left Paris = I propose quitting Paris on friday Night for London & meet the Vessel at Lymington as Mr Robinson will do all the necessary arrangements at Southampton ...[85]

[Postscript] My sincere thanks to yr Lordship for the recommendation of Lord Orford wh whom I hope to do business when he returns in the winter – also for the recommendation of Lord Cassilis – but his Lordship has not yet paid me a visit & I do not know his Lordship's address.[86]

James Nixon is recorded in directories between 1816 (the Rate Books record him in 1815) and 1835 as a cabinet-maker and upholsterer, with premises at 123 Great Portland Street. From 1835 he traded as James Nixon & Son, but clearly (see p. 30) his son was working with him from at least 1830. The latest entry for James Nixon & Son is in Pigott's directory of 1839. So far all that is known of James Nixon's trade is gathered in the entry for him in the *Dictionary of English Furniture Makers*.[87] In 1835 a directory described his trade as being exactly that testified to by the few references in the Stuart papers: 'importer of foreign marbles and ancient furniture', and the *Dictionary* also records the mention of him by J.C. Loudon as one of the tradesmen who hold 'curious and ancient furniture, including fragments...and rearrange these curious specimens and adapt them to modern use'.[88] In 1842 the architect William Burn (1789-1870) was advising his client Onesiphorus Tyndall Bruce to go to 'Nixon & Co for old oak carvings' for the furnishing of Falkirk House, Fife.[89] Nixon's first recorded dealings with Lord Stuart de Rothesay were in relation to Carlton House Terrace and the supply of marble. On 5 May 1829 Lord Caledon wrote to his brother-in-law: 'Nixon has set your chimneypieces very well and I have bought some from Him of an inferior kind which he is putting up in the bedrooms'.[90] It seems to have been the London house that was entirely occupying him at this time. Decimus Burton wrote on 11 November 1829 about the finishing of the parquet and sounded a little exasperated with his client: 'the work generally having been so much divided by his Lordship's direction during the last twelve months between Messrs Bennett & Hunt [91] and Mr Nixon I confessed I could not decide until I had referred to former documents, which of them should do this portion of the work'.[92] He continued, sounding a little put-out: 'Mr Nixon was employed by his Lordship without any contract that I was aware of.' In 1830 Lord Caledon refers to Nixon's success at papering and painting, for which he will use him on his own house too.[93]

References to Nixon in papers of other families are sparsely recorded as yet, but further bills may be hoped for. We know that in 1833 Nixon was supplying chimneypieces to the Duke of Buccleuch.[94] Only one piece of furniture so far identified as having been made by Nixon (and for an unrelated commission) is a table at Castle Ashby, in the Rococo Revival style. It carries a label of Nixon & Son, indicating a date after 1835. However, it seems likely from Loudon's description of his trade that he was making, selling and restoring furniture of all periods and techniques and creating much of it from fragments of earlier pieces. Certainly he was submitting a drawing of 'Dwarf bookcases & of the sideboard to be placed opposite the fireplace' to Lord Stuart on 18 June 1830.[95] In the trading line we have the evidence of a letter from H. J. Nixon Jr to Lord Stuart on 30 July 1830: 'I have cleared the Tables ex Serlie[?] which arrived last week valueing them at 22.10. -'.[96] This suggests that the firm was acting once more as agents in the importation of furniture.

The Nixons were undertaking exactly the same trade as the dealer Edward Holmes Baldock (1777-1845) in Hanway Street, London.[97] They must have been but two of several such operators in the London trade at the time.[98] It is reasonable, given what has been published on Baldock's methods and his talents at 'composing' furniture, to suggest that it may have been Nixon who supplied the dressing-tables by Schlichtig and Bircklé which have undergone such clear alterations (F.22, F.23), the boulle table with its new 19th century frame (F.21) and the 'dragon' table (F.20).[99] If we look at similar pieces known to have been made up by Baldock however, we have to admit that Nixon was, from these examples, demonstrably less skilled at the work. However, though no bills from Nixon have so far been traced, Lord Stuart de Rothesay's bank account shows that between 5 December 1833 and 13 December 1836, 25 payments were made to one or both of the Nixons, or on their orders, the total amounting to almost £1500.[100]

If we know little of Nixon we know even less of Gunn, but it is possible that they worked regularly together. We know that Gunn was not merely a shipper, that he had other clients, as his letter suggests, and that he did sell furniture, ormolu and textiles, as we learn from a bill of 1838 to the Duke of Sutherland:

Bt. of S[sic] Gunn, Rue Amelot, No. 64	
11 Dec. 1838	
A Library Table	Fr. 1,000
Secretaire of Marie Antoinette	Fr. 150
1 Gilt Vase	Fr. 150
1 Pr Bronze tripods	Fr. 600
1 Pr of Oak Leaf Holders for fire irons	Fr. 200
6 pieces of Savory for screens	45/
	Fr. 270
Total	Fr. 2,370.00[101]

In 1839 Gunn made his only appearance in printed records, in Bottin's *Almanach du Commerce*, where he was listed as at the same address in Paris, with the classification *curiosité*. In the classified section, under *Curiosité, objets d'art, medailles* he is listed most particularly:

Gunn (Geo), pour l'angleterre, anciennes marbres princip[alement] cheminée et statues du siècle de Louis XIV, Objets d'art, curiosité, bronze,

pendules, boiseries sculptées, meubles de marqueterie r[ue] N[euve]
Vivienne, 49 et [rue] Amelot, 64, b[oulevard] St Antoine.[102]

Though he did not appear in the editions of 1833, 1835, 1841 or 1843, the listing here of two addresses suggests a large business indeed and significantly one directed to his fellow Britons. This raises the question of his clientele. Clearly he sold to individuals but to what extent was he supplying British dealers such as Nixon and, indeed, perhaps Baldock? During the 1830s and 1840s Paris was a rich market for furniture, panelling and all sorts of objects from which the collectors' market was created, but the money to purchase such objects was concentrated in London, the capital of a rapidly developing industrial and trading economy. Mr Gunn was capably exploiting the opportunities of trading from one capital to another.[103]

It was probably Nixon rather than Gunn about whom John Smith was writing on 20 July 1829 to James Loch, the agent for the Sutherlands, but we cannot be sure.

> I called today at York House – the Grand Staircase may now be said to be
> completle [sic] finished and I took a Gentleman with me who has seen most
> of the fine things on the Continent and at Paris particularly whither he goes
> on Thursday – bt Stafford House surpases [sic] all that he has seen, for
> grandeur as a whole, and for fine substantial workmanship in particular –
> the last he much admired – he is fitting up a house for Lord Stuart de
> Rothesay and Lord Caledon in Carlton Garden, and some other relations
> of Lord Harwicks [sic], and imports nearly all the fine French marbles that
> are imported.[104]

In an undated letter filed with those of 1832, January to August (though it possibly should be dated 1831), Gunn writes from a cholera-stricken Paris about several items which appear to have been missing from the cases sent to Lord Stuart. Though items are not so clearly described as to be identifiable, the nature of those that Gunn was sending is clear. He writes specifically of a marble vase (another one has been promised 'to prevent any dispute with Mr Gregory'). He explains that four pieces of marble for the doorway had never been made and asks Lord Stuart, who holds the drawings, to forward them. Clearly Mr Gunn was obtaining and despatching large-scale commissions of new work and possibly some of the architectural salvage already referred to. He writes in the same letter of '4 door tops with dragons' which have been packed and forwarded, and the descriptions of these are reminiscent of the dragon-supported table (F.20), though none of the overdoors are visible in the 1942 *Country Life* photos of Highcliffe. When he lists the possible cases in which they might be found (nos 312 or 534) we can understand the scale of the work that he was undertaking for Lord Stuart. Case 312 contained a *desus[sic] de Porte* and the legs of an oak table; case 534 contained carved frames and carved wood. It is in this letter that specific reference is made to the porcelain-mounted cabinets (F.19), and the full reference is quoted in that entry. In the same letter Gunn suggests how wide were his commissions when he mentions that he had ordered

34   500 walnut trees for his client. Gunn asks to be paid in London because of the situation in Paris, suggesting that he came and went freely.[105]

On 30 December 1832 Gunn was again writing from Paris, from the rue Amelot, about various matters.[106] He was clearly still amassing pieces for Stuart. He writes: 'Martin, from the rue Peppiniere has this moment delivered to me a Nicepaire … [illegible in the manuscript] to be forwarded to your Lordship'. He mentions the keys for 'Lady Stuart's Inlaid Consoles' (F. 19) and writes 'as soon as I get yr Lordships directions the wood, glass etc., shall be despatched.'

On 12 January 1834 George Gunn wrote again:

> I beg to acknowledge the receipt of yr Lordship's three last Letters & in reply to inform yr Lordship that Article deliverd by Martin & calld by him a Necessaire proved to be a Lot of Silver dishes etc. for Breakfast or Luncheon wh Cut glass etc etc which has been duly forwarded to the address of Lord Berwick via Havre. Wd yr Lordship's instruction to Mr Lefebvre etc – the glass shall be forwarded to Prince Talleyrand – it is now at Havre waiting further orders – the wood etc is also ready but the water in the Seine is so very high that no Steam Boats have left Paris for the last 2 months and as we continue to have heavy Rains I fear it will be some time before they will reach Hvre – I am truly happy to acquaint your Lordship that I have at last laid my hands on the 13 Suits of State Livries so long lost – and I want yr Lordships directions as to forwarding the same – they have been laying at the Roulage ever since without any number or address – and as the Roulage makes a clear out every 3 years of all such cases I attended as a forlorn hop to xamine every case opened – & thank God I have found them all safe and <u>now</u> in <u>my possession</u>. No doubt in the hurry of quitting the Embassy Sottorconnolli [a servant ?] sent them by a Commissionaire to the Roulage the Evening of I January 1831 waiting yr Lordships directions…[107]

Gunn was still doing business with Stuart in 1837; a letter to Stuart from a Charles Okey in Paris (possibly a colleague from the embassy days), dated 4 December, reads: 'The reply to the enquiry for Gunn is that he is is London'. This letter makes it clear that Okey was still acting for Stuart in Paris as he had been in the early 1830s, and he throws in a final question: 'I want your Lordships orders about the vases'.[108]

So far only one further reference to Gunn has been traced, in the fictional account of the real life of the Baronne de Feuchères, mistress of the Duc de Bourbon, by Violet Stuart Wortley. She refers to the purchase by the Baronne (Sophie Dawes, from the Isle of Wight) of an aristocratic Italian title from a man called Gunn. Bearing in mind Mrs Stuart's careful reference to letters as the source of her other works of family history it is possible that this had a source in family papers, probably now untraceable.[109] If true, it even further widens the range of commodities in which Gunn traded.

The extent of the consultation with Paris and the purchasing from Paris can only be guessed from the scattering of letters that survive, interleaved with correspondence on government affairs during the 1830s. In 1833 Hamilton Hamilton, a diplomatic colleague, wrote from the Paris Embassy on 11 February about his projected return to England, during which he was to act as courier for cases of items being sent to Stuart.[110] Six years later a letter dated 19 January 1839 to Mr Okey in Paris complains of non-payment of a debt of 2043 fr. by Lord Stuart de Rothesay. It is signed 'Ringuet, Paris', the well-known cabinet-maker.[111]

In 1841, it was Lady Stuart who was providing for Highcliffe in Paris. A letter from Jn Apley [?] runs:

> The Porcelain your ladyship wants is extinct, there were large sets of it once but it has been so dispersed and to make up a set, if possible, could require a long time to search and it would now be very dear. It is asked for <u>how many</u> the service is required. Lord G's is green if I recollect with gold etc. Will the modern <u>best</u> white & gold service of the pattern do? and for <u>how many persons</u> about? the people in the FB St Germain keep large stocks of modern and not dear. Lord Cadogan shown [sic] how great difficulty in getting together a set of the old Sèvres which often ... any set complete.
>
> The people here say that French Bronzes now are worth 100 fr. ...in Russia than here. I mention this as if your lordship likes them, then will ... no less than they are disposed of at your departure.[112]

Stuart was possessed with the idea of his house at Highcliffe. With his father's experience it was surely folly to build on the site, but he set about it with gusto. Initially the idea had been to extend the house which had been built on the old site by Penleaze, the intermediary owner. Stuart commissioned the architect William John Donthorne (1799-1859) who worked in the office of Jeffry Wyatt from 1817-20, where he acquired a facility in the designing of Gothic detailing and some adventurousness in picturesque planning. In the Wyatt practice he had worked on Ashridge, Hertfordshire,[113] when Jeffry Wyattville was completing the vast Gothic house first enlarged by James Wyatt, 1808-13, and on the seaside *cottage ornée* of Endsleigh in Devon, built for the Duke of Bedford in 1810. It is said that Donthorne kept copies of drawings for these when he left the practice in 1820.[114] In his own practice Donthorne designed in both Classical and Gothic styles, but after 1830 concentrated exclusively on the Gothic.[115] The grand project of Highcliffe seems to have started in earnest in the early months of 1830, the last payments for land on the site being recorded only in July 1828.[116] A letter of 8 July 1828 from a M. Robertson, then in Liverpool, refers to Stuart's new appointment to France which 'will postpone the building plan for a while'.[117] It is not clear to which house this refers but mention in the same letter of the purchase of large quantities of 'Timber from the Coast of Africa' suggests the Highcliffe project, where much panelling had to be pieced out and made up. In 1829 and 1830 work was going on at Carlton House Terrace.[118] By 7 January 1830 Donthorne was writing to Lord Stuart with a detailed statement of his views

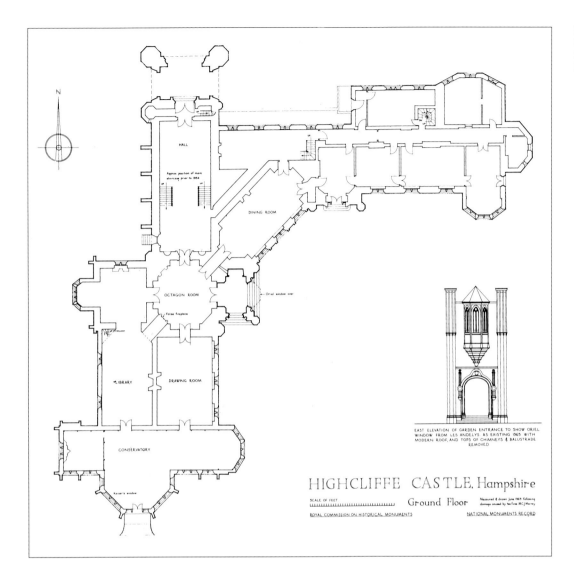

Fig. 12
Plan of Highcliffe Castle.
Royal Commission on
Historical Monuments

36

on the treatment of the hall at Highcliffe and the letter makes clear that this was one step in a regular exchange of views.[119] Stuart was ready to start building.

Highcliffe was substantially finished in 1834, though work continued on the interior throughout the 1830s. It was an enthusiastic and catholic amalgamation of styles. The exterior was in the Gothic style, designed as the vehicle for the architectural fragments that Stuart had acquired in such large quantities during the 1820s in France and was continuing to acquire in the course of the building. Stone carvings were supplemented and extended by details cast or moulded in Roman plaster. Stuart did not confine himself to one period, and the result at Highcliffe was a spirited patchwork, with fragments of Renaissance arabesque carving framing some windows and the most flamboyant Gothic elsewhere. The house was L-shaped (fig. 12), managing to cover an immense amount of ground for relatively few rooms. The main entrance was formed of a porte-cochère reminiscent of Fonthill, announcing the importance of the house in the loudest possible architectural voice.

Donthorne had had little previous experience of using architectural fragments, a habit which was to catch on quickly and widely. Stuart was active in his buying at the moment when the trade in such materials across the Channel was becoming a flood.[120] His position as British Ambassador would have made him particularly susceptible to criticism and it may have been Stuart who was uppermost in the mind of Victor Hugo in the latter's tirade against

Fig. 13
Highcliffe Castle, the Great Hall, looking towards the Tree of Jesse window, and showing the carved panelling from the Abbey of Jumièges

the despoilers of Jumièges, published in 1825, *Guerre aux Demolisseurs!*[121] There Hugo clearly identifies the villains as 'les anglais', who had bought the rights to any of the architectural salvage for 'trois cent francs'. Stuart's role in the actual destruction of the buildings was probably non-existent, but what is clear is that the presence of a ready market for architectural fragments, then as now, can have done little to deter those who favoured demolition.

Stonework and woodwork were accompanied by stained glass, though not usually from the same sources. The glass at Highcliffe was extremely varied. The most impressive piece was the Tree of Jesse window of 1547 from the church of St Vigor at Rouen, which was built into the large window over the main door but within the porte-cochère (fig. 13).[122] On 7 January 1830 Donthorne wrote to his client about the form of this window, pointing out 'which ever window may be adopted over the Door and in the Hall must be new except the glass'.[123] As often happened at Highcliffe and elsewhere, the original glass was not suffcient for its purpose, and had to be pieced out with more modern work. Lady Waterford wrote of the process of piecing it out with modern glass and other fragments of old – she apparently taking part in the process – the leading and cutting being undertaken by the firm of Holloway of Christ Church.[124] The most important of the stained glass was only recognized in this century, two half roundels and a section of border from one of the 12th century windows of Saint-Denis. When Highcliffe became derelict, this glass was removed for reasons of safety and stored. In 1989 some panels were bought by the Victoria & Albert Museum independently of this Bequest (see Appendix, p.100).

In the letters of 1832 there is one reference to a proposed visit to Eastnor Castle, Herefordshire, the home of Lady Stuart's sister who had married Viscount Eastnor, later Earl Somers, but no note of whether or not this took place.[125] Certainly Stuart de Rothesay must have visited at some time and would have found it much to his taste. It was built between 1811 and 1820 to the designs of Sir Robert Smirke, but was incomplete at the death of Earl Somers in 1841. From 1846 Pugin produced designs for the interiors for Crace & Co., and it remains one of his most important surviving commissions.[126] However, when Stuart visited (which he surely did, if not on the occasion cited) it was the theatrically Gothic exteriors which he would have admired.

38   The story of Lord Stuart de Rothesay's own involvement with A.W.N. Pugin is told by Benjamin Ferrey. Pugin was called in to give a second opinion when Stuart's faith in Donthorne wavered. On 28 December 1835 Pugin arrived for a visit of inspection. The radical nature of his suggested re-building obviously unnerved Stuart, and he objected to such wholesale proposals. At this Pugin abandoned the project and departed the next morning.[127] He did not spare Donthorne when he wrote:

> the architect Mr Donthorne could not have had the slightest idea of Gothic architecture as he has turned Norman capitals upside down to serve for bases to the latest style of Louis 12 and Francis I and made a sad havoc with everything.[128]

Fig. 14
Highcliffe Castle, the Great Hall, looking towards the stairs, showing the mosaic floor possibly by Crovatto and the tapestries said to have come from the collections of the Knights of Malta

    The work on Highcliffe dragged on. In 1839 a letter to Lord Stuart from Paris, signed Crovatto, was concerned with 'le dessin du pavé venitien que l'on pourrait éxécuter dans votre pièce avec une bordure gothique les armoiries et le chiffre au milieu' ['the drawing for the Venetian pavement which might be executed for your room with a Gothic border and the monogram in the middle'].[129] It seems likely that this mosaic floor was similar to the one finally executed for the hall and visible at the foot of the stairs in fig.14.

    The organic growth of Highcliffe may have delighted Lord Stuart but it presented horror and increasing worry to his wife. She protested and certain changes and diminutions were made, but Lady Stuart still declared Donthorne 'totally unfit to plan a house...I wish the whole thing would fall over the cliff' when she visited in 1834. [130]

    The ecclesiastical scale of the whole (and the medieval ecclesiastical sources of many of the details of stonework and woodwork) reflect the Stuart of the 1830s, seduced by the glamour of the Middle Ages, anxious to underline the antiquity of his line in the face of a very recent elevation to the peerage.[131] His choice of title was said to have annoyed the King (for the Duke of Rothesay is one of the subsidiary titles of the Prince of Wales), but for Charles Stuart it underlined his illustrious descent. The exterior and interior of Highcliffe were dotted with the Stuart arms, his crest and monogram. Like many 19th-century landowners of much less grand lineage, he (as the son of a younger son) faced a distinct lack of family portraits. Not deterred, he set about making good this deficit. In 1832 his cousin, Lord Wharncliffe, wrote to him 'W: Thompson having left this morning for Liverpool...He has made two capital copies for you of

Fig. 15
Highcliffe Castle, the
Octagon Room, fitted with
'Louis XV' *boiseries* and
marble door frames, almost
certainly from those
supplied by George Gunn

Fig. 16
Highcliffe Castle, the
Drawing-Room, with
Régence boiseries

40 Lady Mary and the Turk Wortley and is as quiet and respectable a man as one could wish to have in one's house.'[132]

Inside the house the architecture of the Great Hall was decidedly Gothic, but most of the other rooms of which we have record in the photographs of *Country Life* (figs 13-19) show panelling, plasterwork and marble door surrounds. At the time these would have been described as 'Old French', indicating the promiscuous mix of French styles from the century before the Revolution, which had returned to fashion in the 1820s, when Louis XV *boiseries* were bought for the Grand Reception Room at Windsor Castle.[133] The Duchess of Rutland was one pioneer in this fashion, starting work on the project for the Elizabeth Saloon at Belvoir in 1824 with similarly imported panelling.[134] In the years that Lord Stuart de Rothesay was building Highcliffe the opulent scheme of interior decoration for the Waterloo Gallery at Apsley House had just been completed.[135] Lord Stuart de Rothesay might naturally have emulated his former commander but he would also have been conscious of other interiors such as Stafford House which demonstrated this style at its most extravagant and powerful.[136] It is not surprising that Lord Stuart chose to follow the taste of his former master, Wellington.

Fig. 17
Highcliffe Castle,
the Dining-Room

The 1949 sale catalogue of Highcliffe makes it clear that Lord Stuart's purchasing for his house was as eclectic as that of any mid-19th-century British aristocrat. Italian *cassoni* and chairs are listed, quantities of the Dutch marquetry which was universally acquired in the middle years of the 19th century, and some 18th century English furniture which may have represented the remnants of a family collection. Amongst the French furniture listed in 1949 are pieces from all periods of the 17th and the 18th centuries. Other pieces had moved from the house earlier, for example a lacquer *secrétaire en pente* stamped 'I DUBOIS' now in the James A. de Rothschild collection at Waddesdon Manor.[137]

The Great Hall, indeed, was dominated by the vast Gothic window and flanked by the Gothic woodcarvings from Jumièges, but its furnishings included Gobelins tapestries said to have been looted by Napoleon from the Knights of St John at Valetta and Italian *cassoni* and large Italianate chairs.[138] The Library too showed somewhat dull Gothic bosses on the ribbed plaster ceiling, but the utilitarian fittings for the very large numbers of books allowed little further reference to period. Elsewhere, the *ancien régime* held sway. From the Hall led the Octagon Room (fig. 15), the walls with 'Louis XV' panelling deriving from designs by

Fig. 18
Highcliffe Castle, the
Library

Fig. 19
Highcliffe Castle, the
Chinese Room, the bed
hung with embroideries
said to have been owned by
Marie Antoinette (T.1)

Nicolas Pineau (1684-1754), the door panels with carvings of various derivation, including some (possibly of lacquer) in the Chinese taste, the door-surrounds of heavy white marble, echoing the opulence of Louis XIV interiors and carved with the arms of Lord Stuart. The Drawing-Room was panelled with a *Régence*/Rococo design, the marble door-surrounds here of coloured marble, the furnishings more dominantly Louis XV. The Dining-Room (fig. 17), leading from the Octagon the opposite way, is, as was accepted practice, more plainly panelled in oak, but the ceiling is a rather perfunctory essay in *Régence* motifs.[139] Of the smaller rooms at least two showed Chinese papers or textile hangings, but these were bedrooms and dressing rooms, as might be expected (fig. 19). Already, by 1840, Highcliffe had settled itself in an established pattern which was to hold good throughout the century, of drawing-rooms in Rococo style with dining-rooms and libraries in a heavier and earlier style. The suave Classicism of the Empire furniture, reminding Lord Stuart de Rothesay of the sophistication of the public rooms in which he spent much of his earlier life, was, by 1840, an anachronism, not due for revival for another half century. The likelihood is that it was his death, and the abandonment of the house in Carlton House Terrace, that brought this Classicism to rest amongst the 'Old French' of Highcliffe.

The creator of Highcliffe had little time to enjoy more than the building of his great dream. In 1841 he was sent abroad once more on diplomatic service and when he returned in 1844 he was already a sick man, dying the following year.

42   NOTES FOR PAGES 19-41
NLS: National Library of Scotland

8. Robert A. Franklin, *Lord Stuart de Rothesay* (1993) was a surprisingly late first biography of Charles Stuart, which provides the most accessible account of his complicated diplomatic life. The *Dictionary of National Biography* provides a succinct listing of his many appointments.
9. Violet Stuart Wortley, *Magic in the Distance,* (1949), pp.162-3.
10. Violet Stuart Wortley, *Highcliffe and the Stuarts,* (1927), p.7.
11. Violet Stuart Wortley, *Highcliffe and the Stuarts,* op. cit., p.133.
12. Violet Stuart Wortley, *Highcliffe and the Stuarts,* op. cit., p.193.
13. The best account of the Embassy is found in Mary Beal and John Cornforth, *British Embassy, Paris. The House and its Works of Art,* (1992).
14. Joseph Friedman, *Catalogue of the Bonaparte Borghese collection of furniture and bronzes,* (1985).
15. Roger Boutet de Monvel, *Eminent English Men and Women in Paris 1800-1850* (London: David Nutt, 1912) and J. G. Alger, *Napoleon's British Visitors and Captives 1801-15* (London: A. Constable & Co., 1904).
16 Violet Stuart Wortley, *Highcliffe and the Stuarts,* op. cit., p.236.
17. Mary Berry (1763-1852) and her sister Agnes, the friends of Horace Walpole. See *The Dictionary of National Biography.*
18. *A Second Self.* Letters of Harriet Granville 1810-45, ed. Virginia Surtees (1990), p.242.
19. For a description of the Stuart's involvement in the ball see Violet Stuart Wortley, *Magic in the Distance,* op. cit., pp.199-200.
20. Lady Morgan, *France in 1829 and 1830* (London: Saunders & Otley, 1831), vol. I, pp.147-52.
21. NLS MS 21311 f.97. Francis, the second son of Lady Conyngham, was at one time attached to the Embassy in Paris under Sir Charles Stuart.
22. Christophe Leribault, *Les anglais à Paris au 19e siècle* (Paris: Editions des Musées de Paris, 1994), pp.25-32.
23. NLS MS 21268 ff.109-111. The Cercle Français was not formally founded until 1824. Christophe Leribault, op. cit., p.30.
24. Violet Stuart Wortley, *Highcliffe and the Stuarts,* op. cit., p.x.
25. Mary Beal and John Cornforth, op. cit., p.38.
26. PRO T1 4067, transcribed in Joseph Friedman, *British Embassy – Paris: the history of a house 1725-1985* (1985), vol. 3, pp.31-7.
27. Michelot is listed in directories of Paris as *marchand de meuble* at 41 rue de Argenteuil.
28. Joseph Freidman, *British Embassy – Paris: the history of a house,* op. cit., vol. 3, p.60, but without reference to source.
29. *French Connections. Scotland and the Arts of France* (Edinburgh: HMSO; Royal Scottish Museum, 1985) pp.55-70.
30. F.J.B. Watson, 'Walpole and the Taste for French Porcelain', in *Horace Walpole, Writer, Politician and Connoisseur, essays on the 250th anniversary of Walpole's birth,* ed. W.H. Smith (New Haven/London: Yale, 1967), p.329 and S. Eriksen, *Early Neo-classicism in France* (London: Faber & Faber, 1974), pl. 238.
31. Eileen Harris, 'The Moor Park Tapestries', *Apollo,* LXXXVI (1967), pp.180-88.
32. Christopher Gilbert, *The Life and Works of Thomas Chippendale* (London: Christie's/Studio Vista, 1978), pp.36-7.
33. Ibid.
34. *Carlton House. The Past Glories of George IV's Palace,* 1991, *passim.*
35. John Cornforth 'Inverary Castle, Argyllshire I and II', *Country Life,* CLXIII, (1978), pp.1619-22, 1734-37.
36. J. Mordaunt Crook, 'Broomhall, Fife', *Country Life,* 29 January 1970, pp.242-46.
37. Sotheby's, 12 June 1992, lots 299-310.
38. J. Mordaunt Crook, op. cit. p.245.
39. Roger Boutet de Monville, op. cit., *passim.*
40. BM Hardwicke Papers 35,395. The Earl of Clancarty (1767-1837) had been Stuart's predecessor as Minister at The Hague and returned there in 1816 as Ambassador to the new kingdom.
41. NLS MS 21301, *passim.*
42. *Carlton House,* op. cit. pp.37-40 and *passim.*
43. Ibid., cat. nos 21 and 65.
44. Ibid., cat. no. 55.
45. *George IV and the Arts of France* (London: Buckingham Palace, the Queen's Gallery, 1966), *passim.*
46. John Cornforth, 'French Genius in Regency Taste', *Country Life,* 24 March 1966, pp.650-52.
47 Clive Wainwright, *The Romantic Interior* (1989) p.287, plate 264.
48. *French Connections,* op. cit., pp.84-92.
49. For this study it was not possible to search all the papers of Lord Stuart de Rothesay, most of which are not ordered and listed. A list of the main deposits is included in the Bibliography. Many of the deposits relate to his diplomatic life, but the long series of papers in the National Library of Scotland contains some personal papers among others on subjects of public business.
50. NLS MS 15386 f. 28. René Simier (d.1826) was appointed binder to the Empress in 1809. Daniel Alcouffe, Anne Dion-Tenenbaum, Pierre Ennès eds., *Un Age d'or des arts décoratifs 1814-48,* 1991, p.532.
51. NLS MS 15386 f.79.
52. NLS MS 15386 f.179.
53. NLS MS 15387 f.138, 142 and *passim.*; also MS 21265 f.48.
54. NLS MS 21265 f.61.
55. NLS MS 21268 f.149.
56. NLS MS 15387 f.34 and *passim.*, f.43.
57. NLS MS 15387 f.259.
58. The son of the MP for that county and a fellow collector of Spanish books.
59. NLS MS 21267 f.90,128.
60. BM Add MSS 37983 f.23, 40880 f.216, for letters of 1830 and 1832, but the spasmodic correspondence was already well established.
61. No copy of the first is listed in the British Library Catalogue. This does list a copy of the second, *Fragmentos de hum cancioneiro inedito que se acha na livraria do real collegio dos nobres de Lisboa impresso a'custa de Carlos Stuart, socio da academia real de Lisboa em Paris no paço de sua magestade,* the binding of which bears Stuart's own arms.
62. Violet Stuart Wortley, *Highcliffe and the Stuarts,* op. cit., p.viii.
63. NLS MS 15388 f.148.
64. NLS 21316 f.41. Macpherson harks back to the Scottish MSS which he had obtained in Rome in 1799.
65. *Catalogue of the valuable library of the late Rt Honourable Lord Stuart de Rothesay...* S. Leigh, Sotheby and John Wilkinson...31 May 1855. There is an annotated copy in the British Library.
66. NLS MS 21267 f.148.
67. NLS MS 13388 f.81.
68. Lady Stuart to her mother, quoted in Augustus Hare, *The Story of Two Noble Lives,* (1895), I, p.115. On p.116 she records that they paid £25 for it. Quintin Crauford (1743-1819) had long been known to Sir Charles Stuart and had assisted him in the purchase of the Hôtel Charôst. The sale of his picture took place in Paris on 20 November 1820 and the following days.
69. *A Second Self,* op. cit., p.188.
70. For the most accessible account of the house see Christopher Hussey, 'Highcliffe Castle', *Country Life,* XCI (1942), pp. 807-9, 854-7, 902-5.
71. Charles Nodier and J. Taylor, *Voyages pittoresque et romantiques dans l'ancienne France – Normandie* (1820-25), pp.127-33. The plate was re-published in Wainwright, op. cit., pl. 45. Nodier was an antiquarian and bibliophile and may well have been known to Sir Charles Stuart.
72. *Architectural Antiquities of Normandy by John Sell Cotman; Accompanied by Historical and Descriptive Notices by Dawson Turner* (London: John and Arthur Arch; Yarmouth: J S Cotman, 1822), pl. XV.
73. The fate of the stonework from the abbey is treated at length in Eustace Remnant, 'The Problem of the Cloister of Jumièges', *Journal of the British Archaeological Association,* vols XX-XXI (1957), p.107-8.
74. Remnant, op. cit., p.109, records that date for the death of the last exploitative or negligent owner. After that period efforts were made to preserve as much as had survived of the site.
75. Quoted by Remnant, op. cit., p.111.
76. Ibid.
77. NLS MS 21300 f.75.
78. NLS MS 21299 ff.35, 18.

79. Lord Stuart's brother-in-law who was also building on the adjacent site.
80. Violet Stuart Wortley, *Highcliffe and the Stuarts* , op. cit., p.319. The letters about Carlton House Terrace are quoted pp.303-06.
81. London County Council, *Survey of London*, XX, 'Trafalgar Square and Neighbourhood' (St-Martin-in-the-Fields, Part III), 1940, p.83. In 1961 a report by Sir John Summerson (copy in the files of the *Survey of London*) stated that nothing important remained of the original fittings and the interior was subsequently entirely re-modelled.
82. NLS MS 6246.
83. 'Labiois aîné, marbrier, [rue] Amelot 12' was listed in Bottin's *Almanach du Commerce* in 1831. He was recorded as having obtained a 'mention Honorable' at the 1827 *Exposition des Produits de l'Industrie* in the Louvre. I am grateful to Côme Remy for this reference.
84. Auguste-Louis-Joseph Casimir de Franquetot, Marquis de Coigny (later Duke) and General Sebastiani had served together in military and diplomatic life under the Napoleonic regime and almost certainly both knew Stuart. *Dictionnaire de Biographie Français*, vol. IX (Paris: Librairie Letouzey et Ané, 1961).
85. It may have been this statement that caused the date to be interpreted as 1831, but Stuart may have been travelling as part of his (not always wise) diplomatic involvement in the abdication.
86. NLS MS 21309 f.128. Horatio Walpole, Earl of Orford (1783-1858), of Wollerton Hall, Norfolk. He had served with Stuart in both St Petersburg and Madrid. Archibald Kennedy (1770-1846) was created Marquess of Ailsa in 1831.
87. Geoffrey Beard and Christopher Gilbert (eds), *Dictionary of English Furniture Makers 1660-1848* (1986), pp.649-50.
88. J. C. Loudon, *Encyclopaedia of Cottage, Farm and Villa Architecture* (1835), p.1039, 1101.
89. Scottish Record Office MS GD 152/58/2/6, quoted in Wainright, op. cit., p.60.
90. NLS MS 21302 f. 121.
91. Listed in *The Post Office Directory,* 1831, as builders in the Horseferry Road.
92. NLS MS 21304 f.93.
93. NLS MS 21306 f.54.
94. Information from John Cornforth. Nixon writes of 'a large assignement of chimneys on the Road...Hanby purchased a large quantity of goods in Paris...' on 30 September 1833.
95. NLS MS 21307 f.20. Unfortunately the drawings do not survive with the letter.
96. NLS MS 21307 f.93.
97. Geoffrey de Bellaigue, 'Edward Holmes Baldock', *Connoisseur*, CLXXXIX (1975), pp. 290-99, CXC (1975), pp.18-25.
98. Wainright, op. cit., pp.26-53 gives a comprehensive account of the trade of

such firms.
99. Ibid.
100. I am very grateful to Mrs B. J. Peters, archivist of Coutts & Co., for providing me with this information. Despite Gunn's mention of the Nixons in 1831 or 1832, no payments to them were made so early, nor are payments to Gunn listed.
101. Staffordshire CRO D593/Q/1/3. I am very grateful to my colleague James Yorke for providing me with a transcript of this bill.
102. *Almanach du Commerce* (Paris: Bottin, 1841). I am indebted to Côme Remy for tracing this reference for me.
103. This disparity of the markets was pointed out to me by Clive Wainright.
104. Staffordshire CRO D593/K/1/3/19. For this transcription too I am indebted to James Yorke.
105. NLS MS 21310 f.79.
106. NLS MS 21311 f.125.
107. NLS MS 21313 f.7.
108. NLS MS 21315 f.98.
109. Violet Stuart Wortley, *Sophy, the Winkle Picker*, (1941) p.159.
110. NLS MS 21312 f.13.
111. NLS MS 21316 ff. 19, 20. Julien-Daniel-René Ringuet (1777-1839) was in partnership with his adopted son, Auguste-Emil, as upholsterers and makers of furniture. See Denise Ledoux-Lebard, *Les Ebénistes du XIXe Siècle* (1989), p.555. It is just possible that Ringuet could have made the pair of cabinets (F.19) and the table referred to in that entry.
112. NLS MS 21317 f.95. Lord Stuart de Rothesay was about to depart as Ambassador to St Petersburg. The illegibility of much of this letter is frustrating.
113. Wainright, op. cit., pp.67-8.
114. Roderick O'Donnell, 'W.J. Donthorne (1799-1859): architecture with "great hardness and decision in the edges"', *Architectural History* 21 (1978), p.83.
115. The classical house which he built on the site of the dower house of Highcliffe at Bure Homage for the Baroness de Feuchère in the 1830s is illustrated in O'Donnell, op. cit., pl. 29b. Presumably the introduction for that house came through the Highcliffe connection.
116. NLS MS 21300 f.80.
117. NLS MS 21300 f.77.
118. NLS MS 21303-6, *passim*.
119. NLS MS 21307, f.2.
120. The best account of the development of the trade in architectural fragments and of the interiors that derived from them is found in Wainright, op. cit., chapters 2 and 3.
121. Victor Hugo, *Oeuvres Complètes* (Paris, 1882) I, p.320, quoted in Wainright, op. cit., p.57.
122. Jean Lafond, 'La Peinture sur verre à Jumièges', *Congrès scientifique du XVIIIe Centenaire de Jumièges*, II (Rouen: Lecerf, 1954) p.508.
123. NLS MS 21306 f.2.

124. Hare op. cit., I, p.175-80, quoted from Lady Waterford's reminiscences.
125. NLS MS 21310 f.118.
126. Giles Worsley, 'Eastnor Castle, Herefordshire I' *Country Life* CLXXXVII (1993), pp.82-5; Clive Wainwright, 'Eastnor Castle, Herefordshire II', *Country Life* CLXXXVII (1993), pp.90-3.
127. Benjamin Ferrey, *Recollection of A.W.N. Pugin and his Father Augustus Pugin* (re-published London: The Scolar Press, 1978), pp. 190-93. I am grateful to Clive Wainwright for confirming the date of this visit.
128. Phoebe Stanton, 'Sources of Pugin's "Contrasts"', *Concerning Architecture* ed. J. Summerson (London: Thames & Hudson, 1968), p.121.
129. NLS MS 21316 f. 45. In Bottin's *Almanach du Commerce*, op. cit., Crovatto is recorded in 1832,1833 and 1835 as a maker of mosaic and a stucco worker in the avenue Boufflers, no. 7; in 1839, 1841 and 1843 he is listed as a maker of mosaic at 11 rue Monsieur, though in the listing under name in 1843 he is described as in partnership with Henri Bex and in the listing under trade he is described as 'stucateur de la couronne et des princes de la famille royale', this indicating the quality of his work.
130. Quoted in Roderick O'Donnell, op.cit., p.88.
131. Margaret B. Freeman, 'Late Gothic Woodcarvings from Normandy', *Metropolitan Museum of Art Bulletin*, vol. IX, No. 10 (1951), pp.260-69. J.H. Powell, 'Highcliffe Castle, near Christchurch, Hampshire', *Transactions of the Ancient Monument Society*, XXV (1967), pp.82-94. Roderick O'Donnell, op. cit., pp.83-92.
132. NLS MS 21311 f.122.
133. John Martin Robinson, 'The North State Rooms, Opulence and Ingenuity', *Apollo*, CXXXVIII (1993), p.126.
134. James Yorke, 'Belvoir Castle, Leicestershire, I and II, *Country Life,* CLXXXVIII (1994), no. 25, pp.89-93, no. 26, 62-5.
135. John Hardy, 'The Building and Decoration of Apsley House', *Apollo*, XCVIII (1973), pp.12-21.
136. John Cornforth 'Stafford House Revisited' I and II, *Country Life* CXLIV (1968), pp.1188-91, 1257-61.
137. Geoffrey de Bellaigue, *Waddesdon Manor, Catalogue of the Furniture and Gilt Bronzes* (Fribourg: Office du Livre, 1974), no.62.
138. Christopher Hussey, op. cit. III, p.903.
139. Donthorne wrote about the panelling of this room to Lord Stuart in 1833, recording that the plain panels were designed to take family pictures. NLS MS 21312 f.71.

The Arrangement
of the Handbook

The pieces are listed under the Collections to which they were assigned and are numbered with the following alphabetical prefixes:

F   Furniture & Woodwork

M   Metalwork, Silver & Jewellery

P   Prints, Drawings & Paintings

C   Ceramics

S   Sculpture

T   Textiles & Dress

A   Appendix

Books from the National Art Library are listed alphabetically by author but are not numbered.

The furniture and furnishing bronzes are all catalogued and illustrated, as relating to the purchasing of Lord Stuart de Rothesay. All other items have been treated in handlist form, with illustrations of a representative number of pieces which derive from his collection. The jewellery, which was largely Lady Abingdon's own, has been similarly listed and several pieces are illustrated.

The Appendix notes three further items, not part of the Bequest. These are fragments of panels of 12th-century stained glass, removed from Highcliffe, which came to the Museum in 1989. Their importance and their association with Lord Stuart de Rothesay's collecting prompts their inclusion, though no detailed discusssion is possible here.

FURNITURE & WOODWORK

Furniture from Highcliffe

The furniture of the Bettine, Lady Abingdon Collection represents in microcosm the extensive purchases of Lord Stuart de Rothesay. Though no 19th-century inventories of Highcliffe have been traced it is likely that the contents remained substantially as bought by him. His daughter, Lady Waterford, had several other properties, including Ford Castle in Northumberland, and spent only part of the year at Highcliffe.

Most of the furniture is of the Empire period, the style of furnishing which had surrounded Sir Charles Stuart during his early working life. In the first decade of the 19th century a strong, smooth Classicism in interiors had proclaimed the Empire throughout mainland Europe. The restoration of the monarchy in France modified but did not overthrow this style. It seems clear that Stuart retained a fondness for the Parisian glamour which had dazzled him as a young man. It must also have suited well the interiors of his house in Carlton House Terrace in the 1830s.

The acquisition of pieces once belonging to Maréchal Ney (F.5,6,7) seems to have been prompted by admiration for a hero, though they may also have reminded him of one of the grandest Parisian houses of the Empire period. The Hôtel de Saisseval (in the rue de Bourbon, later the rue de Lille) had been purchased by Ney in 1805 to consolidate his social position. Napoleon had engineered suitable marriages for several of his marshals to create for himself an imperial establishment.[1] Ney's wife (daughter of a former lady-in-waiting to Marie Antoinette) was amongst the most successful of all in creating an elegant and remarkable house.[2] The inventory taken after Ney's death certainly reveals a highly fashionable interior, including a *boudoir argenté* hung with yellow taffeta and furnished with silvered wood and bronze.[3] Stuart must have known and admired it. We may regret that he acquired only the simpler, mahogany chairs from the Petit Salon, but it is likely that he acquired these 'relics' for his own use, perhaps in a study.

Also represented in the Bequest is the plain, good-quality furniture of the *Restauration* which Stuart must have bought for family use. The 1949 sale catalogue of Highcliffe lists many small tables and commodes similar to F.17 and F.18.

Both in London and for Highcliffe it seems clear that he was buying primarily to furnish. His contact with the collecting *coterie* in Paris seems not to have bred in him any developed connoisseurship of furniture. The two 18th-century dressing-tables (F.22 and F. 23) illustrate the sort of pieces which fed the new collecting trade in Britain (see p. 24) and with the two other tables (F.20 and F.21) document the extent of alteration, elaboration and creation which such pieces frequently underwent.

The grant of arms (F.24) does not relate to Lord Stuart de Rothesay but is included here as part of the Bequest to the Furniture & Woodwork Department.

The acquisition of this furniture considerably strengthened the Museum's holding of the Empire and the *Restauration* periods, but its true importance lies in its provenance. It documents the contemporary, or near-contemporary purchasing of a francophile Briton of French furniture for domestic use, and the development, in the course of his lifetime, of an aristocratic convention of collecting French furniture of earlier generations.

F.1
Pair of Armchairs *(Bergères)* **and a Settee** *(Canapé)*
French, 1805-10, by Jean-Baptiste-Bernard Demay
Mahogany; seat rails of beech; upholstery not original
a,b stamped 'DEMAY/RUE*DE*CLERY'
c unstamped, the cross pieces under the seat marked in pencil 'VI'
a,b H: 94cm W: 74cm D: 62cm
c H: 93cm W: 135cm D: 62cm
Accession nos: W.9a,b,c-1987

Fig. 20
F.1 *Bergère*, one of two, with a *canapé*, by Jean-Baptiste-Bernard Demay, 1805-10

Jean-Baptiste-Bernard Demay (1759-1848)[4] married the daughter of the *menuisier* Claude Sené (1724-92) and was granted his *maîtrise* in 1784, continuing his father-in-law's workshop from about 1806. He worked for the Garde Meuble Imperial producing much high quality furniture, specializing in carving in mahogany and often using, as here, carved motifs in place of gilt-bronze mounts. These large-scale winged monopodia relate to a *fauteuil de bureau* supplied by Jacob-Desmalter in 1805 for Malmaison.[5] A similar chair appears in a portrait of the Emperor in his study at the Tuileries by Isabey, beside a table with similar supports.[6] In this, Demay was following a form also supplied by his father-in-law.[7]

F.2
Pair of Armchairs (Fauteuils)

French, 1810-20, by Jean-Baptiste-Bernard Demay
Mahogany; the seat rails of beech (some renewed); upholstery not original
b stamped under the front rail
'DEMAY/RUE+DE+CLERY'
H: 90.5cm W: 61cm D: 56cm
Accession nos: W.6a & b-1987

These chairs are of strong design although without gilt-bronze mounts, in the manner often employed by Demay. A *fauteuil* in the

Fig. 22
F.2 Stamp of Demay on the seat rail

Louvre with exactly the same design of front legs and uprights in one piece, based on the design of antique swords, is stamped by Jacob-Desmalter and labelled for the Tuileries.[8] The structural upholstery of the two chairs seems to have been done at different times, although they have been given matching coverings. The original seat upholstery would seem to have been higher, leaving no visible gap between the seat and the back. A matching chair, also stamped, from the estate of Lady Abingdon, was sold at Christie's, London, 10 December 1987, lot 95.

F.3
Island Bookcase (Etagère)

French, 1810-15, by Jean-Georges Hornig
Mahogany on a carcase of oak and poplar; the capital mounts chased and gilt, the handles probably lacquered brass; slab of *rosso antico* marble
Inscribed in pencil on the wooden backing

to the slab 'hornig ébéniste/ rue Charonne no. 7'; a faint inscription may read '1810'; scratched figure 'I' on top of the carcase
H: 78cm W: 49.5cm D: 37cm
Accession no: W.22 b-1987

Jean-Georges Hornig (1779-1857) is recorded in the rue de Charonne in 1827.[9] This form of small open bookcase seems to have been his speciality, the only type of furniture recorded as being made by him. A similar one, unmarked, was sold at Christie's, London, 29 March 1979, lot 72, and this is attributed to Hornig by analogy with two others which are said to carry the same marking (mark not illustrated).[10] The dated inventory mark on F.4, also attributed to Hornig, suggests that he was making this type of furniture more than a decade earlier than has previously been recorded. The form of these low bookcases seems to derive from the cabinets in boulle marquetry made from 1770-95 by Etienne Levasseur (1721-98).[11] On the bookcases similar corner pilasters are retained, here flanking books rather than the drawers or doors of the Levasseur pieces.

47

Fig. 24
F.3 Inscription of Hornig on the wood under the marble slab

Fig. 21
F.2 *Fauteuil*, one of two from a set of seat furniture by Jean-Baptiste-Bernard Demay, 1810-20

Fig. 23
F.3 Dwarf bookcase by Jean-Georges Hornig, 1810-15

48

Fig. 25
F.4 Dwarf bookcase attributed to Jean-Georges Hornig, 1810-15

F.4
Island Bookcase *(Etagère)*
French, 1810-15, attributed to
Jean-Georges Hornig
Mahogany on a carcase of oak and
poplar; chased and gilt mounts; slab of
grey granite
Under the slab, paper label printed with
the arms of Stuart and inscribed 'Sir
Charles Stuart'; heart-shaped paper label
inscribed 'No. 50 / Une petite Table Carré
/ en dessus de Marbre / en cuivre doré /
Paris ce [le] 20 août / 1816'. The carcase is
inscribed in pencil on the top 'No.2'
H: 78cm W: 49.5cm D: 37cm
Accession no: W.22a-1987

This piece is attributed to Hornig by
analogy with F.3. The two, clearly treated
as a pair, are shown in the *Country Life*
photographs of the Library at Highcliffe,
flanking the chimneypiece in 1942. They
do not figure in the 1949 sale.

The labels on this piece are the best-
preserved of two varieties of label that
appear in fragmentary form on many
pieces in the collection. The small label
printed with the Stuart arms almost
invariably appears with the larger heart-
shaped labels, suggesting that the latter is
likely to relate to an inventory made for
Sir Charles Stuart. As many of the labels
are damaged, its absence now on some

pieces with the other label is no indication
that it was not there originally. The heart-
shaped labels are close to those found on
the furniture listed in the 1814 inventory of
Pauline Borghese's furniture in the Hôtel
Charôst.[12] Such labels are not recorded
elsewhere. Though Pauline had left France
by 1816 the question must remain open
whether Sir Charles Stuart obtained some of
her simpler furnishings for personal use,
perhaps through an agent.[13] Another
possible explanation is that Sir Charles
Stuart, recognizing the necessity for making
an inventory of his own possessions
employed the same agent, Michelot. Such
labels may turn out to be a speciality of this
furniture broker.[14]

F.5
Three Armchairs *(Bergères)*
French, *c.* 1805, by Jacob-Desmalter, for
Maréchal Ney for the Petit Salon of the
Hôtel de Saisseval, Paris
Mahogany, with chased and gilt mounts;
seat rails of beech, some renewed; the
upholstery not original
b and **c** stamped 'JACOB D
                  R MESLEE'
b carries unreadable paper label inside back
rail
c carries paper label inside back rail, with
ink inscription 'Marechal Ney'
H: 96cm W: 66cm D: 61cm
Accession nos: W.2a, b, c-1987

In the inventory of his goods taken after the
execution of Maréchal Ney, started on 27
December 1815, the contents of 'Une pièce
servante [de] Petit Salon' at the Hôtel de
Saisseval included a suite of seat furniture
'acajou, satin bleu brochée, figures
égyptiennes en bois et cuivre d'oré' ['in
mahogany, blue brocaded satin, egyptian
figures in wood and gilt bronze'].[15] The
whole suite was valued at 900 fr. It comprised 2 large *bergères*, 2 smaller *bergères*,
2 other *bergères*, 2 *fauteuils*, 4 *chaises*, 2
tabourets en X and 1 *tabouret de pied*.

In the *bail* or rental agreement drawn up
between Madame la Princesse de Moskowa,
Ney's widow, and the Comte de Peralada,
the Spanish Ambassador who rented the
house from February 1816 to April 1817,
the contents of the Salon Bleu are listed as 4
fauteuils, 4 *bergères*, 4 *chaises*, 1 *canapé*, 2
tabourets de pieds and 1 screen, all in
mahogany with gilt-bronze mounts,
upholstered in 'etoffe de soie fond bleu et
chamois' ['silk fabric with a blue ground

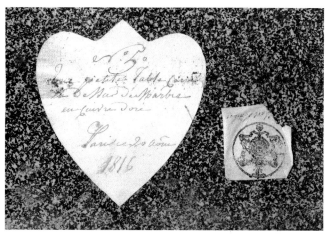

Fig. 26
F.4 Labels under the granite slab, probably relating to an inventory made for Sir Charles Stuart of his personal furniture in 1816

and buff colour'], with case covers in silk lined with *toile royale*.[16] Though the number of pieces differs it is probable that the same set is being described.

The furniture must have been sold from the *hôtel* after the lease of the Spanish Ambassador expired. As there is no traceable public sale of the furniture of Maréchal Ney, it is possible that Sir Charles Stuart bought these pieces from his widow as a private transaction. Stuart, like many of his contemporaries, showed his admiration for Ney, and he was distressed that he had to stand aside in the matter of the marechal's execution.

Another *bergère* from this set is in a private collection, on loan to the Bowes Museum, Barnard Castle. The early history of that chair is not known, but it is thought to have been in the collection of Maréchal Canrobert, a hero of the Second Empire, and may have been acquired by him also in memory of 'the bravest of the brave'. That *bergère* is slightly smaller than these three, following the listing of two sizes in the inventory. It too has lost its original upholstery.

The firm of Jacob Desmalter[17] was the largest supplier of fine quality furniture in the period of the Empire. Its founder, Georges Jacob (1739-1814), may have learned his trade of *menuisier* from Louis Delanois (1731-92). He established his workshop in 1765, the year he was granted his *maîtrise*. Before the Revolution he was much occupied with work for Queen Marie Antoinette, but his friendship with the painter David ensured the successful continuation and development of the firm during two further generations, when carcase furniture was made as well as carved furniture. The firm became in turn official suppliers to the Directorate and to the Empire and its clients included most of the imperial marshals. In 1803, on the death of his eldest son, Georges Jacob (who had turned over the running of his firm to his sons in 1796) re-entered a partnership with his second son, François-Honoré-Georges (1770-1841), as Jacob-Desmalter et Cie., which lasted until the end of 1828. This form of stamp was used by the partnership of Georges Jacob with his second son, 1803-13.

Fig. 28
F.6 Chair, one of two from the set supplied *en suite* with the *bergères*

49

F.6
Pair of Chairs (*Chaises*)
French, *c.*1805, made by Jacob-Desmalter, for Maréchal Ney, for the Petit Salon of the Hôtel de Saisseval, Paris
Mahogany, with chased and gilt mounts; seat rails of beech; the upholstery covering modern, the structural upholstery original
Stamped under the front rails 'JACOB D
                                    R MESLEE'
Paper labels inside the back rails inscribed: 'Marechal Ney / Petit Salon', label on **b** additionally inscribed '/20'
H: 91cm W: 48cm D: 45cm
Accession nos: W.10a & b-1987

Fig. 27
F.5 *Bergère*, one of two, from a set supplied by Jacob-Desmalter in about 1805 for the Petit Salon of the Hôtel de Saisseval, the Paris house of Maréchal Ney

50

Fig. 29
F.6 Stamp of Jacob-Desmalter on the seat railsa

For the record of these chairs in the inventory of the goods of Maréchal Ney see F.5. These chairs have retained their original structural upholstery with wide (10cm) webbing (woven with a stripe), set close together in the French fashion. Under the present top covering the backs show the sharp-edged *à tablette* upholstery which originally would have been highlighted by cording or braid. The maker's label of destination helps to date the chairs quite closely. Ney acquired the Hôtel de Saisseval in March 1805 and almost immediately began its remodelling and furnishing. Certainly the furniture must have been supplied between 19 May 1804 (when Ney was made a maréchal) and 6 June 1808 (when he was granted the title of Duc d'Elchingen). Jacob-Desmalter would have been punctilious in observing the correct form of address for such an important client.[18]

F.7

Pair of X-Framed Stools *(Tabourets en X)*
French, c.1805, made for Maréchal Ney, for the Petit Salon of the Hôtel de Saisseval, Paris, almost certainly by Jacob-Desmalter
Mahogany, parcel gilt with lacquered brass mounts; seat rails of beechwood (renewed); stretchers of stained beechwood (possibly renewed); upholstery not original.
Paper labels on slips of wood inside long rails read 'Mr Le Ml / Ney / Petit Salon', one label semi-illegible
H: 56cm W: 63cm D: 41cm
Accession nos: W.4a&b-1987

For the record of stools in the Petit Salon of the Hôtel de Saisseval in the inventory of the goods of Maréchal Ney and for their dating, see F.5 and F.6. The different iconography of these stools, with their leopard heads rather than the sphinx heads of the *bergères*, might suggest a separate origin in the house, but if the evidence of the label is accepted it is likely that they were also made by Jacob-Desmalter although any stamp has been lost with the replacement of the rails (the paper labels have been cut out with a slip of wood and re-applied to the new rails). One of the

stools is illustrated in the 1942 *Country Life* articles on Highcliffe, in the Chinese Dressing Room, at the foot of a mahogany bed with gilt-bronze mounts said to have belonged to Maréchal Ney.

The stools are a version of those supplied for the Consulate at the Tuileries, *c*. 1800 by Jacob Frères.[19] The form was often repeated for the imperial palaces. In 1811 stools of a similar form were supplied by the firm for Malmaison.[20] The original line of the upholstery would have been hard-edged, in the shape surviving on the chairs (F.6).

Fig. 31
F.7 Stool, one of two from the same set of seat furniture

F.8
Cabinet (*Bas d'armoire*)
French, *c.*1805, made by Jacob-Desmalter, possibly for Maréchal Ney, for the Petit Salon of the Hôtel de Saisseval
Mahogany with chased and gilt mounts; carcase of oak with one pine shelf, the interior stained; slab of white marble not original

Stamped on top right of carcase
'JACOB D
R MESLEE'
The carcase is marked on top in pencil 'No 19'. The slab is marked in pencil underneath 'TALL BUREAU'
H: 93cm W: 90cm D: 71.5cm, excluding marble
Accession no: W.21-1987

This cabinet is of a standard Empire form but the quality of the craftsmanship is of the highest found among the regular productions of the workshop. It is tempting to relate it to the seat furniture (F.5-F.7), though it carries no label. However, in the 'Pièce servante ..Petit Salon' at the Hôtel de Saisseval there was recorded in the 'Inventaire après décés' of Ney a 'Petit armoire en acajou, figures égyptiennes'.[21] That piece is described as having a top in red Italian marble, a colouring much more suited to this handsome piece, which has clearly lost its original slab. We should note in addition the treatment of the Egyptian heads which, allowing for the difference in scale, is very close to that on the *bergères* (F.5).

The large mount of the wreath had been used earlier by Jacob Frères for a large library cabinet and is found on two filing cabinets (*serre-papiers*) by Jacob-Desmalter supplied in 1810 for the Emperor's grand cabinet at the Grand Trianon.[22] The small floret mounts found on the pilasters (and which also occur on the chairs F.5, F.6) occur very widely on furniture by Jacob-Desmalter.[23] The main frieze mount is found on a number of pieces by Jacob-Desmalter at the Palais de Compiègne.[24] It is also found on a jewel cabinet supplied by Jacob-Desmalter in 1810 for the cabinet de toilette of the Empress Marie-Louise at the Tuileries.[25] The roundel mounts above the Egyptian heads have lost their centres but in a list made in 1978 on the death of Lady Abingdon, these were recorded as lion's head mounts.

51

Fig. 32
F.8 Cabinet, by Jacob-Desmalter, about 1805, probably supplied for the same room as the seat furniture (F.5-F.7)

F.9

Four Armchairs *(Fauteuils)*

French, 1803-13, by Jacob-Desmalter
Gilded beech; two with original
upholstery under modern covers
Stamped under the front rails 'JACOB D
R MESLEE'
Paper label inside each back rail, printed
with the arms of Stuart and inscribed in
ink, 'Sir Charles Stuart KB'. W.3a&b-1987
and W.5-1987 also carry on their back rails
a heart-shaped paper label inscribed with
varying fragments of the inscription:
'127/16 fauteuilles en bois d'oré / en Soiye
Vert desseins blanc / avec housses / Paris le
20 août / 1816'. On W.3b the back seat rail
also carries the paper label printed in script
'Uphold.../A.../123', a fragment of the
label of the dealer James Nixon of
123 Great Portland Street
H: 96.5 cm W: 65 cm D: 63cm
Accession nos: W.3a & b-1987
W.5a & b-1987

These chairs relate to parts of lots 130 and
131 in the 1949 sale, but notes on Lord
Abingdon's copy of the sale catalogue

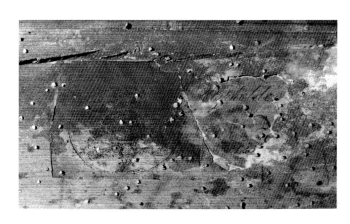

Fig. 34
F.9 Fragment of the
label of the British
upholsterer James
Nixon, 123 Great
Portland Street, on one
of the set, possibly
added about 1830 in
connection with the
shipping of the chairs

indicate that they were bought in. Both
lots were assemblies of giltwood chairs
of Empire style united by matching
fabrics. Lot 130 included 4 *bergères*, a pair
of *fauteuils* and another 'similar', with 2
other *fauteuils* which are described as
having semi-circular crestings. All are
described as having 'original green silk
damask with medallions, formal foliage
and strapwork in silver' (which follows
the description on the chair labels of the
upholstery in 1816). Lot 131 included

Fig. 33
F.9 *Fauteuil*, one of
four from a larger set
by Jacob-Desmalter in
the possession of Sir
Charles Stuart by 1816

fauteuils, armchairs and foot stools, all in
'old pink damask with a design of Cupids,
doves, drapery and floral festoons and
foliage' (similar to the present upholstery
of **W.5a & b-1987**). The first part of this
lot was a set of four *fauteuils* described as
having 'winged Egyptian heads', which
sound very similar to the pair of *bergères*
and four *fauteuils* which figure at the head
of lot 130. One pair of *fauteuils* in Lot 131
is annotated in Lord Abingdon's copy
of the catalogue 'swan design', which
suggests that the matching of sets for the
two lots was done entirely on the colour
of the fabrics and not on the details of the
carved decoration.[26] The total of pieces
from the 'Egyptian heads' suite listed in
lots 130 and 131 seems to have been 2
bergères (possibly 4, depending on
interpretation of the term 'armchair' and 8
(or 10) *fauteuils.* Lot 130 is described as
having come from 'Madame la Maréchale
Ney, Princesse de la Moskowa, wife of the
maréchal and originally from the Petit
Salon, Paris', while lot 131 is described as
'formerly the property of Prince Joseph
Bonaparte'. There is no entry in the Ney
inventory to correspond exactly with the
Egyptian heads set. In the Salon Vert there
were only 4 *fauteuils* and 4 *chaises* in
giltwood (with no further description). In
the Grand Salon there were 14 giltwood
fauteuils and 4 *bergères*, but the covering
was gold and 'amaranth'. Elsewhere were
further sets of giltwood seat furniture, but
in each case the identification is not clear.
The Joseph Bonaparte provenance is
equally unproven.

These chairs are similar to the pair F.10,
which are a simpler version of the same
design (unstamped). All carry the same
label referring to a set of 16. This label,
dated 1816, could suggest that the green

upholstery was done at that time to unify them, perhaps for Sir Charles Stuart (but see entry for F.4). We know that one of the principal *salons* of the Embassy was called the Grand Salon Vert in 1814 but this retained its original seat furniture covered in green velvet.[27] It is possible however that Lord Stuart de Rothesay wanted to supplement this furnishing in 1816 for his grand schemes of entertainment. Although there is evidence of some patching to the gilding, they have not been re-gilded. W.3a & b-1987 have been entirely re-upholstered but W.5a & b-1987 appear to have their original webbing, close-set in the Continental fashion.

The label of James Nixon, the London upholsterer, is likely to have been added in about 1830 when Nixon was working with Stuart's Paris agent, Gunn, in shipping the collection to England. Earlier notes on pieces from the collection suggest that the full label text was for 'James Nixon', thus indicating a date before 1835 when he went into partnership with his son (see pp. 30-31).

F.10
Pair of Armchairs (*Fauteuils*)
French, 1803-13, attributed to Jacob-Desmalter
Gilded beech; upholstery not original
Not stamped. **a** carries paper label inside back rail printed with the arms of Stuart and with the ink inscription 'Sir Charles Stuart KB' (over another label), and another, heart-shaped, inscribed in ink 'Seize fauteuils de Bois dor fond vert dessein blanc avec housse. Paris le 20 Aout 1816'. **b** shows traces of similar labels
H: 92.5cm W: 60.5cm D: 60cm
Accession nos: W.7a & b-1987

These are a simpler (unstamped) version of the design of F.9, though clearly they were treated as one set as early as 1816. They are slightly smaller in size, the arms are less decorated and do not carry arm pads, and the back uprights carry only three channels of fluting, rather than the four on the others. The bosses on the seat rails are plain roundels rather than quatrefoils and the detail of the Egyptian heads and the palmette decoration below them are simplified in the design and are carved with less detail, as are the lotus heads at the junctions of the arms and the back. However, it is not impossible that two

closely similar, though not identical, patterns of chair could be used in the same interior. The gilding has undergone restoration in the past and the upholstery is renewed. The webbing is uncoloured, open set in the English fashion.

The similarity of elements of F.9 and F.10 to many other sets of seat furniture supplied by Jacob Frères and Jacob-Desmalter makes identification from inventories and accounts particularly difficult. The motifs were widely used by

Fig. 35
F.10 *Fauteuil*, one of two, from a larger set in the possession of Sir Charles Stuart by 1816, unstamped but attributed to Jacob-Desmalter

the firm of Jacob from *c.*1800, both for mahogany chairs and for giltwood.[28] These are close to a set of seat furniture now at Malmaison, in the Salon de Compagnie, originally supplied for Saint Cloud.[29]

53

Fig. 36
F.11 Console table, one of a pair by
Pierre-Benoit Marcion, 1800-15

54

F.11
Pair of Console Tables
French, 1800-15, by Pierre-Benoit Marcion
Mahogany with giltwood, on oak; frieze
mounts of chased and lacquered brass; slabs
of white marble
Each stamped twice 'P.MARCION'
on the back uprights
b is marked in pencil on the centre strut
of the top 'I'
H: 96cm W: 104 cm D: 32.5cm
Accession nos: W.13a & b-1987

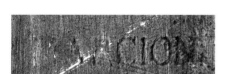

Fig. 37
F.11 Stamp of Marcion on the back of
one of the tables

Pierre-Benoit Marcion (1769-1840)
practised as a cabinet-maker between the
years 1798 and 1817, firstly in the rue
Neuve-des Petits-Champs and later in the
rue Helvetius and the rue de Choiseul.[30]
He was one of the principal suppliers to
the imperial household, second only to
Jacob, and supplied also to several of
the close members of the imperial
establishment, including the marshals.
Pauline Borghese used Marcion, with
others, to furnish the Hôtel Charôst and
Ney's neighbour in the rue de Lille,
Maréchal Mortier, also acquired furniture
by this workshop.[31] The 1814 inventory of
Pauline Borghese's furniture describes
several *consoles* of this type, but the
descriptions are not detailed. Marcion's
furniture was of fine quality, but lacking
the flair of Jacob's best designs. At this
period techniques of mass-production

were being developed in these larger
furniture workshops, and it appears that
the veneering of this piece may have taken
place before it was dis-assembled to be
sent to the carver, for his work on the
capitals at the head of the legs.

F.12
Pair of Armchairs *(Fauteuils)*
French, 1815-25
Beechwood stained to imitate mahogany,
with carving imitating mounts; new
coverings over original upholstery
Unmarked
H: 94cm W: 58.2cm D: 52cm
Accession nos: W.8 & a-1987

In various generations of re-upholstery
these chairs have lost their sharp outline of
seat and back, originally upholstered *à
tablette*, with hard edges outlined with
cord or braid. They do appear, however, to
retain their original webbing, close-set in
the French fashion. The surface has been
cleaned and re-stained in recent years.

Fig. 38
F.12 *Fauteuil*, one of a pair, 1815-25

F.13
Set of Ten Chairs (*Chaises*)
French, 1800-15
Mahogany, upholstery not original;
seat rails of beech
All the chairs carry inside their back rails variously legible versions of the armorial label with the inscription 'Sir Charles Stuart KB' and the heart-shaped label inscribed 'Paris le 20 Aout 1816'. **b** also carries inside the front rail a fragmentary label inscribed '...posés [?] le Maroquin Vert'. **c** also carries the pencil inscription 'No. 2'. **f** and **i** carry inscriptions in ink inside the back rails 'Daille' [?] or 'Dalle' [?] and **g** the inscription 'D'
H: 80cm W: 50cm D: 40.5cm under seat
Accession nos: W.11a-j-1987

The chairs are part of the set of chairs sold as lots 148 and 149 in the 1949 sale. Each of those lots comprised ten chairs but none of the labels on these chairs is sufficiently legible to give the size of the set when it was included in the inventory of 1816. In 1949 they were already upholstered in rexine and the current various upholsteries are more recent. Certainly the *Country Life* photographs of 1942 show a large group of these in the Dining-Room at Highcliffe. The early reference on the label to leather seats suggests that they were always used as dining chairs but their source is not known. At the Hôtel de Saisseval the small dining-room was supplied with 17 mahogany chairs, covered in leather, but in red leather. At the Hôtel Charôst in 1814 the smaller dining-room contained 'vingt deux chaises curulles en acajou et maroquin vert', which might be identified with these and which were not there in 1841.[32] However, the identification remains uncertain.

F.14
Table (*Guéridon*)
French, 1810-20
Mahogany, on a carcase of beech; chased and gilt mounts; the mahogany top is probably a replacement for marble
H: 76cm D: 72cm
Accession no: W.16-1987

The 1949 sale of Highcliffe included several tables of this description but none with matching dimensions. Such small tables with supports featuring Classical heads were a standard form in the first 20 years of the 19th century. A table which may be this one was shown in the *Country Life* photos of 1942, in the window of the Library.

55

Fig. 40
F.14 *Guéridon*, 1810-20

Fig. 39
F.13 Chair, one of ten, from a larger set in the possession of Sir Charles Stuart by 1816

F.15
Console Table
French, 1815-25
Mahogany on a carcase of oak; chased mounts, possibly gilt; slab of *pietre dure* and *marbre de Corse* or Napoleonite
Unmarked
H: 91cm, over slab W: 132cm D: 62.2cm over slab
Accession no: W.12-1987

Though unstamped, this table is of good quality. The taste for fossil marbles was well-established in the first quarter of the 19th century. It was a development of the late 18th century enthusiasm for minerals, shells and other types of natural history materials. It paralleled the taste for native

hardwoods with interesting figure which also became a popular fashion in the early 19th century. The form of diorite used for the centre of the slab of this table was particularly popular in the first two decades of the 19th century. Its origin in Corsica might be interpreted as a compliment to the Emperor, and it was certainly named with this in mind. That Sir Charles Stuart should be interested in such a table is not surprising in view of the large quantities of architectural marbles that he acquired for the building of his house at Highcliffe (pp. 30-33). A smaller console table, of similarly restrained good quality, was sold from the estate of Lady Abingdon (Christie's, London, 10 December 1987, lot 100).

F.16
Fall-Front Secretaire (*Secrétaire à abattant*)
French, 1815-30
Mahogany on a carcase of oak; chased and gilded mounts; slab of white marble (not original)
Stamped on the back right upright with an inventory mark, a shaped cartouche surrounding 'D A' (H: 4.4cm)
H.(under marble): 145cm W: 101.6cm
Accession no: W.24-1987

This secretaire is of a standard form and is of excellent quality. The finely-figured veneers are carefully matched and the combination of carved mahogany and gilt-bronze mounts enlivens the severe outline.

Fig. 41
F.15 Console table, with slab of Napoleonite framed in *pietre dure*, 1815-25

Fig. 43
F.16 *Secrétaire à abattant*, exterior

The mounts in the form of theatrical masks are unusual and of good quality, though unrelated to the more standard floral mounts. The same chased motif of chrysanthemum heads, used here on the capital mounts, appears on the plinths of a pair of candelabra in the Museum's collection (M105-1984) and on a commode sold Sotheby's, New York, 11 October 1995, lot 67.

The inventory mark has not been identified but makes clear that this was not a new purchase by Stuart.

Fig. 42
F.16 *Secrétaire à abattant*, 1815-30, interior

Fig. 44
F.16 Inventory mark (unidentified) on the back of the *Secrétaire à abattant*

58

F.17
Dressing-Table
French, 1820-30
Mahogany, on a carcase of beech, oak
and poplar; lacquered brass mounts; slab
of white marble
Paper label under main drawer inscribed
'assador au 2e De la République' [?].
Under the pen block in the drawer is a
pencil inscription 'from / Dressing Table /
Col Wortley's / Dressing Room'.
Alphabetical inscriptions in pencil on
several of the drawers. 'N1' in ink under
the foot of the mirror
H: 143cm W: 83.8cm D: 43cm
Accession no: W.17-1987

The dressing-table with attached glass was
a form developed in the early years of the
19th century. A particularly spectacular
one was made by Jacob-Desmalter for the
use of the Empress Josephine at the
Tuileries in 1805, and he duplicated the
design in 1811 for the Empress Marie-
Louise at Compiègne.[33] The form with
X-supports is seen at its grandest in a
dressing-table made for the Duchesse

de Berry (who was a friend of the Stuarts,
see p.21) in about 1823 by François
Remond.[34]

Lot 596 in the 1949 sale was a dressing-
table of similar description, but smaller.
The number of pieces of this date and
quality in the sale catalogue supports the
idea that Sir Charles Stuart may have
bought a number of supplementary useful
pieces (such as this and F.18) for use in the
Embassy.[35] The inscription, however, does
not directly support this and is puzzling.
If the Second Republic is referred to (and
this is not clear) then it must have been
a later addition to the collections
at Highcliffe.

F.18
Commode
French, 1820-30
Mahogany on a carcase of oak and poplar;
lacquered brass mounts; slab of white
marble
Drawers numbered in ink with Arabic
numerals
H: 89cm W: 115cm D: 56.5cm
Accession no: W.23-1987

This simple piece is likely to have been
purchased by Sir Charles Stuart during his
second embassy. The mounts are more
floral than classical, suggesting that it was
made in the years of the *Restauration*. It is
clear that the piece has been in constant
use, and the top drawer shows signs of
sub-division and alteration. A closely
similar small writing cabinet was sold at
Sotheby's London on 30 November 1990,
lot 250. It carried the same mounts of
baskets of flowers and the same keyhole
escutcheons and bore the paper label
inscribed 'L.S.de Rothesay' with the
printed armorials (fig.49).

F.19
Pair of Cabinets (*Meubles à hauteur
d'appui*)
French, 1828-30
Marquetry of mahogany with rosewood,
amaranth and other woods on oak,
incorporating the monogram SR; doors
inlaid with porcelain plaques cut from
earlier table wares in mounts of wood or
chased and gilded brass; slabs of *cipollino*
marble, the interiors of the cabinets and

the doors veneered with bird's-eye maple
Paper label on back of each printed with
the arms of Lord Stuart de Rothesay and
inscribed in ink 'L.S. de Rothesay'
H: 98cm W: 74cm D: 46cm
Accession nos: W.18a & b-1987

These cabinets were made during the
second embassy of Lord Stuart de
Rothesay to Paris (1828-31). The
monogram could not have been used
before Stuart was ennobled in 1828.
These cabinets are referred to in a letter by
George Gunn to Lord Stuart de Rothesay
(undated, but in the summer of 1832) in
which he writes: 'most of the little articles
of value belonging to Lady Stuart at the
Embassy were packd in the consoles inlaid
wh Porcelain wh Chipoline Marble tops'.[36]

On 30 December 1832 from Paris he
writes: 'I have not yet been able to get the
Keys for Lady Stuart's Inlaid Consoles –
the Locksmiths here will not part the Keys
from the Locks and I am obliged to send
into the Country for them – as they are
not made in Paris'. Clearly these were
especially favourite pieces, commissioned
to include the monogram, but sadly no
document so far discovered allows us to
know by whom they were made. The
practice of mounting cabinets with
porcelain became very common in the
1830s in Britain, particularly in the work
of brokers and cabinet-makers such as
Edward Holmes Baldock (1777-1845),
who specialized in supplying 'new and
improved' versions of 18th-century French
porcelain-mounted furniture.[37] This pair is

59

Fig. 48 (top)
F.19 Detail of monogram in the marquetry of
the sides, and of the plaques cut from useful wares
in porcelain

Fig. 49 (above)
F.19 Paper label with the arms and initials of Lord
Stuart de Rothesay, on the back of the cabinets

of interest because of the fragmentary
nature of the small pieces of porcelain used
in place of the more usual specially made
plaques. Most appear to be from table
ware in Paris porcelain of various dates
between the 1780s and 1820s. Some appear
to be small plaques specifically made for
the purpose, but most are clearly cut from
the edges of plates (showing the curvature
of the original piece and sometimes the
banding of colour at the edge) or hollow
vessels. In the case of one or two plaques
the curvature is quite pronounced. The
plaques have been selected, with some
balancing of pairs with similar painting or
palette, and the best painted pieces have
been selected for the large octagonal
plaques in the centre of the top and
bottom edges of each cabinet. The
marquetry shows the strong light/dark

Fig. 47
F.19 Cabinet, one of a pair, mounted with porcelain,
made for Lady Stuart de Rothesay, 1828-30

contrast favoured in France in the 1820s. Though they were clearly a special commission, the quality of the cabinet-making is not of the best.

The cabinets appeared as lot 89 in the 1949 sale and at that time were in the Ante-Room to the Library, though the annotations of Lord Abingdon in his own copy of the catalogue record that they were originally in the Blue Bedroom. They were bought in.

The only reference to Stuart's dealings with any French cabinet-maker is the letter from the firm of Ringuet (see p.35). Though Ringuet were known to have worked for English clients there is no evidence that these came from their workshops. A mahogany games table of the same date, with a similar cypher in light wood marquetry on the frieze and 'mounts' in a *Restauration* form but executed in marquetry, was sold at Sotheby's 30 November 1984, lot 377.

F.20
Centre Table
Probably English, 1830-40, incorporating earlier elements of French giltwood and gilt-bronze. Possibly supplied by James Nixon of 123 Great Portland Street

Gilded wood; chased and gilt mounts; the slab of black marble and *pietre dure*
A label under one frieze is printed with the arms of Lord Stuart de Rothesay and inscribed in ink 'L.S. de R.' (as illustrated with cat. no. 21).
H: 92.5cm W: 132cm D: 65cm
Accession no: W.14-1987

The eclectic style of this table represents the most elaborate creations of the dealers such as Nixon (and the more celebrated Baldock – see pp. 31-2), who provided for the new enthusiasm for collecting in the second quarter of the 19th century in Britain, combining elements of old furniture with new and embellishing them with mounts culled from a variety of sources. The dragon legs are finely carved and may derive from a genuine *Régence* table. They are joined by a coarsely moulded x-shaped stretcher, which derives from the design of Louis XIV chair stretchers. The frieze may be partially old and appears rough within; the lower edge of each long side shows an inset section of newer wood and this is carved with a mixture of *Régence* and Rococo motifs, interrupted in the centre of each side with a square gilt-bronze patera, bolted through

the frieze and set in an awkward reserve with an arched top that suggests a circular mount was first intended. These paterae derive from (and may be casts from) original mounts of the Louis XIV period. The sunflower scrolling mount in the recessed panels of the frieze is the same model as the mount found on the frieze of a semi-circular commode of the 1780s stamped 'STOCKEL' in the Museum's collection (W.22-1958), but also on a 19th-century table in the style of Weisweiler sold Christie's, Singapore, 1 October 1995, lot 939. The swan corner mounts are of a particularly strong bulbous form. They would seem to date from the Empire period, but their origin is untraced. The black-ground *pietre dure* slab was probably acquired new for the creation of this table in the 1830s.

In the 1942 *Country Life* photographs of Highcliffe the table is visible to the left of the fireplace in the Drawing-Room, but it is possible that it was originally intended for one of the Chinese rooms at Highcliffe (two Chinese Rooms and a Chinese Dressing-Room are listed in the 1949 catalogue). It is also worth noting that George Gunn, writing in 1832 from Paris to Lord Stuart de Rothesay, mentions that '4 door tops with dragons have been packed & forwarded'.[38] These must also have been for a Chinese interior.

A marble-topped table with dragon supports of identical form, but without a stretcher, was shown in the Lansdowne House Exhibition of 1929, from the collection of Mrs David Gubbay.[39] It was there described as 'Possibly French, Louis XIV', which was presumably what Lord Stuart de Rothesay thought this was when he acquired it. An identical table (almost certainly the same one) was shown in the Saloon at Houghton in 1994 illustrations.[40] However, Lord Stuart de Rothesay may have been seeing in this table a more contemporary and local exoticism. There are precedents for Chinoiserie of this fanciful kind, of course, in Brighton Pavilion, where the work on the Banqueting Room and the Music Room was completed in 1818.[41] Further Chinoiserie rooms were to be created at Temple Newsam (1820s) and Burton Constable (1840s), for which furniture was

Fig. 50
F.20 Giltwood table, probably British, 1830-40, composed of earlier elements

carved by Thomas Wilkinson Wallis of Hull and Louth (1821-1903), in a house which also showed particular influences from France.[42] A table of similar date, also supported on dragon-wreathed legs, was sold by Christie's from Moyns Park on 4 November 1993 (lot 162).

Though there is no evidence of the source of this table, it is exactly the sort of piece that would have been supplied by Nixon, judging by the brief descriptions of his trade that exist.

F.21
Table
Probably English, 1830-40, incorporating the table carcase and top from a French late 17th-century table. Possibly by James Nixon
Ebony and boulle marquetry on a carcase of oak; chased and lacquered brass mounts
Unmarked
H: 76cm W: 63cm open D: 37cm
Accession no: W.15-1987

By the 1830s boulle marquetry was the sign of a serious collector. During the 18th century in France the tortoiseshell and brass marquetry associated with the name of André-Charles Boulle (1642-1732) had remained constantly marketable through all the changes of fashion, and references to it in sales testify to the power of the name. The English collectors had joined in with enthusiasm, led by the Prince Regent and Lord Yarmouth (Stuart's close friend in Paris during his first embassy, later Lord Hertford).

The top, including the drawer section of this piece, is taken from a table of the

Fig. 51
F.21 Table in boulle marquetry, French, 1680-1700, the frame made in England, 1830-40

1680s which would have been supported on a faceted, tapering octagonal shaft above a tripod base (examples of such tables are in the British Royal Collection and the collection of the J. Paul Getty Museum, Malibu).[43] The four stout cabriole legs supplied for the table in the 1830s are derived from French forms of

the 1750s for small tables (particularly porcelain-mounted or lacquer-mounted tables) by the cabinet-maker Bernard Van Risamburgh II (after 1696-c.1766) or Roger Vandecruse (1727-99), but are considerably less delicate in line. The mounts at the tops of the legs are of a Louis XIV pattern.

Though there is no evidence of the source of this table, like F.20 it is close to the sort of furniture that Nixon is likely to have supplied. In the 1942 *Country Life* photographs this table is shown in the centre of the Octagon Room at Highcliffe. It figured as lot 94 in the 1949 sale but was bought in. Lord Abingdon's notes in his copy of the catalogue suggest that it was formerly in the Drawing-Room.

Lord Stuart de Rothesay's acceptance of such altered pieces indicates that although he was in touch with many of the most serious collectors he was himself perhaps most concerned with such pieces as furnishings for his new house.

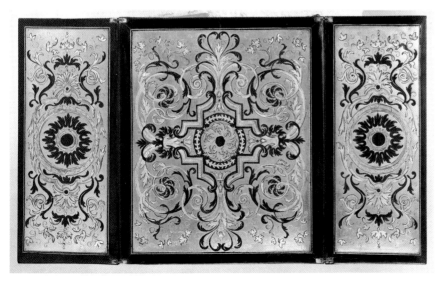

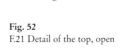

Fig. 52
F.21 Detail of the top, open

62

F.22
Dressing-Table *(Table à dessus brisé)*
French, 1760-70, by Jean-Georges
Schlichtig, with alterations, possibly by
James Nixon in the 1830s
Tulipwood and marquetry including
bird's-eye maple on a carcase of oak and
pine; mounts probably lacquered brass
Stamped under the back rail 'I G
SCHLICHTIG'
H: 73.5cm W: 84 cm D: 49cm
Accession no: W.19-1987

This dressing-table illustrates Lord Stuart
de Rothesay's buying in the most
orthodox fashion of aristocratic furnishers
of the 1830s and 1840s. The elegant lines
and decorative floral marquetry of Parisian
furniture of the 1750s and 1760s had a
particular appeal to women, and it is
possible that this was bought for the use of
Lady Stuart or her daughters. By the time
of the 1949 sale it had lost its function
entirely as a dressing table and had been
absorbed as a 'collectors piece', appearing
as lot 30 in the sale, then shown in the
Drawing-Room, and probably used there
closed, as a writing table. It was bought in
at the sale.
    Jean-Georges Schlichtig (fl. 1765-82)
was one of the many German immigrant
cabinet-makers who flourished in Paris in
the second half of the 18th century.[44] He
was in his 40s when he gained his *maîtrise*
and established himself in the rue du
Faubourg-Saint-Antoine, later moving to

the rue Saint-Nicolas, where his widow
continued his workshop until 1787, a few
years after his death. He worked for Marie
Antoinette on at least one occasion,
providing a commode in the Transitional
style, a style for which he is best known.
The dressing-table has undergone at least
one major overhaul, and the nature and
thoroughness of the work suggests that it
is likely to have been done in the 1830s
and perhaps by James Nixon for Lord
Stuart de Rothesay. The carcase of the
piece has been thoroughly re-built with a
straighter plan, and the marquetry has
been re-applied. The internal structure of
the two hinged flaps, with a mirror set
beneath a panel displaying an 18th-century
pastel portrait of an unknown man, has no
precedent in the 18th century and suggests
the sentimental idea of hidden portraits
which is more in keeping with the taste of
the 19th-century collector. The use of
bird's-eye maple as a lining veneer to the
flaps is also an indicator of the extent of
work in the 1830s, and the presence of a
single-throw lock is equally indicative of
English work. The marquetry has been
scraped to improve the colour and the
detail of the engraving re-inked.

F.23
Dressing-Table *(Table à dessus brisé)*
French, 1765-70, by Jacques Bircklé, with
alterations, possibly by James Nixon in the
1830s
Tulipwood, marquetry and parquetry of

Fig. 53
F.22 Dressing-table, 1760-70, stamped Schlichtig,
with later alterations

Fig. 54
F.23 Dressing-table, 1765-70, stamped Bircklé, with
later alterations

several woods on a carcase of oak; the
escutcheon probably of lacquered brass
Stamped twice under the front rail 'I
BIRCKLE' and 'JME'
H: 70.3cm W: 79.2cm D: 46.3cm
Accession no: W.20-1987

Jacques Bircklé (1734-1803) worked in the
rue Charenton and the rue Saint-Nicolas
producing large numbers of pieces of
medium and high quality.[45] The workshop
was carried on by his son until 1835. Later
in Bircklé's career, nearly 20 years after
obtaining his *maîtrise* in 1764, he began to
supply pieces to the Queen for Saint-
Cloud and to other members of the royal
family. Indeed most of his known work is
in the Transitional or Louis XVI style.
This dressing-table must have been made
early in his career, following the full
cabriole shape of the mid-century. Similar
marquetry, of a trophy of musical
instruments against a cube background, is
shown on a commode by Bircklé.[46] He was
noted for his sparing use of metal mounts.
    This piece would have had the same
appeal for Lord Stuart de Rothesay as
F.22. It has undergone similar but less
drastic work during the 19th century.

In the 1942 *Country Life* photographs it appears in the Drawing-Room, used as a centre table. It was lot 29 in the 1949 sale but was bought in. It was listed there in the Drawing-Room with F.20.

F.24
Grant of Arms to The Earl of Abingdon
English, 1682
Case of leather with gilt tooling, lined with printed paper; the grant of vellum with gilding and polychrome decoration including a portrait of Charles II
Box dimensions H: 9cm L: 97cm D: 9.5cm
Accession no: W.25-1987
James Bertie, Lord Norreys of Rycote,

younger son of Montagu, 2nd Earl of Lindsey, was created Earl of Abingdon on 30 November 1682.

Fig. 55
F.24 Grant of arms to the Earl of Abingdon, 1682, in contemporary case of stamped leather

63

NOTES FOR PAGES 46-63

1. Eric Perrin, *Le Maréchal Ney* (1993), p.118.
2. The full history of the street and its many important houses can be found in *La rue de Lille, Hôtel de Salm*, exhibition catalogue (Paris, 1983). The discussion of the Hôtel de Saisseval is on pp.120-23.
3. A.N. MIN. CXVII, 1082. The best short summary of the descriptions found in the inventory is found in Perrin, op. cit. pp.124-31. In the late 1820s the house (then devoid of furniture) was rented for a year by Lady Blessington, who fortunately made detailed descriptions of its luxurious interiors in *The Idler in France* (London, 1841) vol.I, p.97 *et seq.*
4. Denise Ledoux-Lebas, *Les Ebénistes du XIXe Siècle* (1989), pp.157-61.
5. Alvar Gonzalez Palacios, *The French Empire Style* (London: Hamlyn, 1966), p.111.
6. Madame Basily-Callimaki, *Jean-Baptiste Isabey, sa Vie, son Temps, 1767-1855* (Paris: Frazier-Soye, 1909), p.95.
7. Ledoux-Lebas, op. cit., p.283.
8. Serge Grandjean, *Empire Furniture* (1966), pl.32.
9. Denise Ledoux-Lebard, op. cit., p.263.
10. Ibid.
11. Alexandre Pradère, *French Furniture Makers. The Art of the Ebéniste from Louis XIV to the Revolution* (London: Sotheby's, 1989), p.309.
12. PRO, T1 4067, transcribed in Joseph Friedman, *British Embassy – Paris: the history of a house 1725-1985* (1985), vol. 3, pp.31-7.
13. I am grateful to Madame Ledoux-Lebas and Monsieur Christian Baulez for discussing this matter with me.
14. Michelot is recorded as a *marchand de meubles* at 41 rue d'Argenteuil in 1816.
15. Paris, Archives nationales, Min, CXVII 1082. *La Rue de Lille, Hôtel de Salm*, 1983, pp.120-23.
16. Paris, Archives nationales, AN. VIC. ET-CXVII-1083.

17. Ledoux-Lebard, op. cit., pp.267 *et seq.*
18. The significance for dating of the cabinet maker's labels was pointed out to me by Jean-Pierre Samoyault of the Mobilier National.
19. *Jules et Paul Marmottan, Collectioneurs* (Paris: Musée Marmottan, 1990), no. 100.
20. Hans Ottomeyer, 'Möbel aus Malmaison in München', *Kunst und Antiquitäten*, 3/90, pp.32-40.
21. Paris, Archives nationales, Min, CXVII 1082.
22. Denise Ledoux-Lebas, op. cit., pp.302, 327.
23. Ibid., pp.319,321,326.
24. Svend Eriksen, *Early Neo-classicism in France* (London: Faber & Faber, 1974), pls 36, 51.
25. Colombe Samoyault-Verlet and Jean-Pierre Samoyault, *Château de Fontainebleau, Musée Napoléon I* (Paris: Editions de la Réunion des Musées de France, 1986), p.70. I am grateful to Jean-Pierre Samoyault for drawing my attention to this.
26. The 'swan design' ones (or the pair of *fauteuils* in lot 130 also described as having swan arm supports) may be the ones sold at Christie's, New York, 19 May 1988, lot 221, where they were catalogued as carrying the stamp used by Georges Jacob before 1796. Jean-Pierre Samoyault points out that the form of the front legs is, however, more consistent with a date of c.1810.
27. Mary Beal and John Cornforth, *British Embassy, Paris. The House and its Works of Art* (1992), p.63.
28. Ernest Dumonthier, *Les Sièges de Jacob Frères* (Paris: Editions Albert Morancé, 1921), pls 29, 30, 32, 41. Jean-Marcel Humbert, Michael Pantazzi and Christiane Ziegler, *Egyptomania* (Paris: Réunion des musées nationaux, 1994), pp 280-1.
29. Gérard Hubert, *Malmaison* (Paris: Editions de la réunion des musées de France,1989), p.55. These and other sets are listed in Colombe Samoyault-Verlet and Jean-Pierre Samoyault, *Le Mobilier du Général Moreau* (Paris, Editions de la réunion des musées de France, 1992), p.38. Elements of the same pattern recur on a suite of giltwood furniture supplied to the general in 1802 by Jacob Frères.

30. Denise Ledoux-Lebas, op. cit., pp.461-9.
31. Ibid., p.467.
32. PRO T1 4067 for the 1814 inventory: see note 12. The 1841 inventory is to be found in the *Letter Book of the Architect Decimus Burton relative to repairs etc of HBM Embassy*, 1841-3 (National Art Library, Victoria & Albert Museum).
33. Serge Grandjean, op. cit., pl. 21.
34. Alcouffe *et al*, *Un Age d'or des arts décoratifs* (1991), p.187.
35. Also lots 158,159,160,161,162 and others.
36. See p.33
37. Geoffrey de Bellaigue, 'Edward Homes Baldock' I and II, *Connoisseur*, CLXXXIX (1975), pp.290-99, CXC (1975), pp.18-25. Geoffrey Beard and Christopher Gilbert (eds) *Dictionary of English Furniture Makers 1660-1840* (1986), p.34.
38. NLS MS 21310 f.79.
39. London: Lansdowne House, *Catalogue of Loan Exhibition of English Decorative Art at Lansdowne House, London...*(London, 1929), no. 320.
40. Christie's sale catalogue of items from Houghton, 8 December 1995, p.vii.
41. John Morley, *The Making of the Royal Pavilion* (1984). Geoffrey de Bellaigue, 'Chinoiserie at Buckingham Palace', *Apollo*, 101 (1975), p.382 illustrates similarly kinked dragons on sideboards designed by Robert Jones and made by Bailey and Saunders for the Banqueting Room.
42. Anthony Wells-Cole 'Another look at Lady Hertford's Chinese Drawing Room', *Leeds Art Calendar*, 98 (1986), pp. 16-22. Ivan Hall, 'French Taste in Yorkshire. Furniture at Burton Constable II', *Country Life*, CLIX (1976), pp.1622-4.
43. Charissa Bremer-David, *Decorative Arts. An Illustrated Summary Catalogue of the Collections of the J. Paul Getty Museum* (Malibu: the J. Paul Getty Museum, 1993), no. 57.
44. Pierre Kjellberg, *Le Mobilier Français du XVIIIe Siècle* (1989), pp. 790-4.
45. Pierre Kjellberg, op. cit., pp.69-75.
46. Illustrated, Pierre Kjellberg, op. cit., p.71.

METALWORK, SILVER & JEWELLERY

Metalwork

Lord Stuart de Rothesay was a man of his time in his taste for gilt-bronze. The 1814 inventory of the Hôtel de Charôst, when it was acquired by Stuart at the Embassy, listed 17 chandeliers and 48 candelabra, 19 sets of firedogs and 11 clocks. Such pieces had been a highly important part of the decoration of interiors from the late 18th century, introducing small-scale sculpture into the very decorative details of a room. Pauline Borghese, from whom the building was purchased, certainly appreciated the effect of luxury that such a wealth of gilt-bronze created, and her particular interest in clocks is well documented. The 1949 sale

catalogue of Highcliffe records large numbers of gilt-bronzes and it is clear that Lord Stuart de Rothesay brought back with him this taste for an opulent material.

Unfortunately we have little information on the sources from which he bought, except the enigmatic reference to Russia (see p.35) which unfortunately fails to provide information relevant to a number of fenders (including M.1), which he clearly had made there. It is possible however that some of his gilt-bronzes were bought in London in the 1830s or 1840s, possibly cast and copied from French originals which were already in his possession. His Parisian agent, Gunn (see p.32) was noted in 1839 as a supplier of bronzes, amongst other things, and may have been one important source. The quality of the pieces varies very greatly, suggesting again that he was buying as a furnisher, rather than as a collector, and from several sources. The pieces here are referred to by the customary term 'gilt-bronze', though the base alloy always varied from piece to piece and was usually closer to brass.

Also from Highcliffe is a small group of the small luxury goods known as Palais Royal work – jewellery stands, candlesticks and small boxes made in engraved mother-of-pearl and gilt-brass. A trade in such small items had been established in the shops of the Palais Royal in Paris in the late 18th century, and the group of items here listed suggests that they may represent

the present-buying (whether for herself or others) of Lady Stuart de Rothesay, as may the workbox composed of porcelain plaques, with the label of Feuillet, rue de la Paix (C.16).

M.1

Fender *(Feu à galerie)*

The *chenets* sections French, 1750-60, the balustrade probably Russian, 1841-4.
Gilt-bronze with iron supports
Unmarked, the monogram SR for Stuart de Rothesay
H: 32.4cm L: 128.8cm D: 20cm
Accession no: M.85-1987

The fender is composed of a pair of Rococo *chenets* of the mid-18th century, linked in the 19th century by a balustrade to create an item of fireplace furniture which came into existence in France only in the final decade of the 18th century. The adaptation must have taken place after 1828, when Stuart was granted his barony, and is likely to have been done while he was Ambassador to St Petersburg (1841-4). The solid-cast technique used for the balustrade is characteristic of Russian workmanship. It is interesting that his correspondence for 1841 (quoted p.35) refers somewhat enigmatically to gilt-bronze work in Russia and may record

Fig. 56
M.1 Fender, gilt-bronze, the outer sections French, 1750-60, the balustrade probably Russian, 1841-4

Fig. 57
M.2 Pair of candelabra,
gilt and patinated
bronze, French,
1800-25

his interest in acquiring items there for
Highcliffe. This was one of a group of
such fenders made for Highcliffe, all
composed of 18th century *chenets* joined in
the same manner by gilt-bronze of the 1840s,
suggesting that Lord Stuart de Rothesay had
them made as furnishing kit.[47] They reflect
the fashion in France during the 1830s of
fenders in the Rococo Revival style, with
outer sections modelled on *chenets* of the
period of Louis XV.[48] The monogram is
close to those on the cabinets F.19.

M.2
Pair of Five-Light Candelabra
French, 1800-25, later adapted for
electricity
Gilt and patinated bronze
Unmarked
H: 74cm W: 28.5cm D: 19cm
Accession nos: M.88 & a-1987

These are the most sophisticated examples
of Empire bronzeworking in the Bettine,
Lady Abingdon Collection. They are

finely cast and chased with a variety of
subtle finishes to the gilding to enhance the
details of modelling and chasing. There are
areas of chemical matting. Lot 4 in the 1949
sale was a pair of candelabra of similar
description, with helmet and claw feet, but
approximately 19cm taller. No exact
versions of this model have been traced,
but a similar winged terminal figure is
visible on a pair of wall-lights in the
collection of the Mobilier National
in Paris.[49]

66

Fig. 58
M.3 Pair of candelabra, gilt-bronze, possibly English, 1820-35

M.3
Pair of Four-Light Candelabra, also Convertible as *Jardinières*
English?, 1800-25, later adapted for electricity
Gilt-bronze
Assembly marks
H: 58.5cm, 59cm W and D of each: 42cm
Accession nos: M.91 & a-1987

These were probably intended to form part of a *surtout de table* and for this reason can also be used as *jardinières*. The highly important *surtout de table* attributed to Pierre-Philippe Thomire (1751-1843), bought for the British Embassy in Paris, possibly by Lord Stuart de Rothesay, also shows pierced baskets for the centre-piece and the fruit stands and may have given the Stuarts the idea of acquiring such a set for their own use.[50] The cutting of the pierced areas is quite rough and the quality of the whole pieces is not of the highest. The *bobèches* are close in detail to the bands on the mounted vases, M.8 and it has been suggested that both may have been made for Lord Stuart de Rothesay in the 1830s in London.

M.4
Pair of Candlesticks
English, about 1830-50
Gilt-bronze (?)
Assembly marks under the drip pan of item **a**
H: 40cm W: 15.5cm D: 15.5cm
Accession nos: M.89 & a-1987

The 1949 catalogue of the sale at Highcliffe documents the large quantities of gilt-bronzes that Lord Stuart de Rothesay bought for his house. A pair of closely similar description was lot 601 in the 1949 sale, so it is possible that these were part of a larger set. Though many pieces came from France, and some appeared to have been ordered in Russia, it is likely that others were supplied in London, possibly by or through James Nixon (see pp. 30-31).

M.5
Pair of Candlesticks
French, 1800-25 (**a** probably English, 1830-40), later adapted for electricity
Gilt-bronze
Unmarked
H: 38.5cm Diam: 19.3cm
Accession nos: M.92 & a-1987

These are of the same model though **a** is of an inferior casting, possibly made slightly later, in England, from the French original. The model was a well-known one in 18th-century France, paired with a youth also supporting a child. As early as 1747 the pair was described as being after designs by Corneille Van Clève (1646-1732).[51]

Another pair, in the sale of the possessions of Monsieur de Selle in 1761, appears to have been of the same model, desribed as bought from the sale of the goldsmith Claude Ballin II (master 1688, d. 1754).[52] Other versions of the model appeared in the Randon de Boisset sale of 1777, the Comte du Lac's sale of the same year and the sale of Marigny, Marquis de Menars, in 1782. [53]

In the Wallace Collection are a pair with ungilded male and female figures (F.80

Fig. 59
M.4 Pair of candlesticks, gilt or lacquered bronze, English, 1830-50

Fig. 60
M.5 Pair of candlesticks, gilt or lacquered bronze, one French, 1800-25, the other probably cast in England, 1830-40

M.7
Lamp
French, 1815-30, later adapted for electricity and repaired and re-patinated in England
Patinated copper mounted in gilt-bronze
Unmarked
Base: L: 41cm W: 19.4cm D: 4.5cm
Top: H: 27.2cm L: 39cm D: 15.2cm
Accession no: M.90-1987

In its original form this was an Argand lamp, a form developed in France in the 1780s by the Swiss chemist Aimé Argand (1755-1803), which used a cylindrical wick around a central tube, allowing more oxygen to encourage combustion. The vase-shaped container would have been a reservoir for colza oil, fed by gravity to the wicks at each end of the arms. The small aperture in the moulding just below the reservoir would have housed a small tap to control the flow and thus regulate the height of the flame.

and F.81), a pair with gilded figures (F.30 and F.31) and a pair with two female figures (F.32 and F.33) which, like the V&A ones, are later casts. [54]

Such celebrated models would have been widely cast in the 19th century and available to collectors. Pairs may have been created from a single model in ignorance of the existence of a pendant. Given our knowledge of Lord Stuart de Rothesay's use of dealers such as James Nixon, it seems likely that **a** is an English copy of the French candlestick, made less than a generation later.

M.6
Four-Light Chandelier
French, 1820-30, or English 1830-40, later adapted for electricity
Gilt-bronze
Stamped 'J*' on the underside of the central urn
H: 23.5cm without chains W and D: 43cm
Accession no: M.93-1987

The swan motif used for the arms of this was a common motif in Empire bronze-casting and woodcarving. The quality of this piece might suggest a 20th-century casting, but the huge availability of gilt-bronzes at Highcliffe would have made the need to acquire new ones very slight.

Fig. 62
M.7 Argand lamp, gilt-bronze and patinated copper, French, 1815-30

Fig. 61
M.6 Chandelier, gilt-bronze, French, 1820-30 or an English version of 1830-40

68

M.8
Pair of Mounted Porcelain Vases and Covers
Chinese (Kangshi period), about 1700, the gilt-bronze mounts probably English, 1815-30
Oriental porcelain mounted in gilt-bronze. The jars carry batch numbers in Chinese characters under the rims of the covers
H: 31cm Diam: 21cm
Accession nos: M.105 & a-1987

The taste for porcelain mounted in gilt-bronze was strong in France throughout the 18th century but waned after the Revolution, though it remained strong in England, particularly amongst the circle of the Prince Regent. The jars have been mounted in the mid-18th century manner, i.e. with the lids raised as pot-pourri pots. However, the late Empire style of the mounts suggests a date after 1815. No parallels have been found for the mounts, and it is possible that the vases and covers were given high-quality mounts in England

Fig. 63
M.8 Mounted vase, one of a pair, the porcelain Chinese (Kangshi) about 1700, the mounts probably English, 1815-30

in the 1830s. The working on the bands of the mounts is similar to that on the *bobèches* on the candelabra M.3, which are also arguably English work. The vases appeared as lot 12 in the 1949 sale where they were described as 'Louis XVI vases and covers' but were bought in.

M.9
Mantel Clock
French, the figure 1800-25, the clock movement 1880-1920
Gilt and patinated bronze
H: 31cm W: 16.8cm D: 11.6cm Diam. of dial: 7cm
Accession no: M.86-1987

The figure of Venus is based on an antique original now in the Vatican Museum. In 1797 the sculpture was seized by the French and brought to Paris, which may account for its frequent appearance in miniature form at that time, though it was clearly known in France more than a hundred years earlier when Antoine Coysevox (1640-1720) completed a marble version in 1686 for the north parterre at Versailles, from which the Kellers brothers cast a version in bronze for the Château de Marly in about 1700.[55] Such small-scale figure sculpture was used on chimney-pieces and commodes. Similar figures are known in the Musée Marmottan, Paris and the Royal Pavilion, Brighton. The adaptation of the figure for a clock was made much later.

M.10
Watchstand and Watch
French, 1770-80, with German porcelain and a Swiss watch movement
Gilt-bronze and porcelain, the figure in contemporary hard-paste Meissen porcelain, the flowers in Sèvres soft-paste porcelain

Backplate of watch engraved 'Goodman, London 29871', for the retailer
H: 30.5cm W: 17.2cm D: 10.2cm
Watch: H: 7cm W: 5cm D: 2.5cm
Accession nos: M.87 & a-1987

The creation of items made from a variety of materials both new and old and rare was the speciality of the French *marchands-merciers* who flourished in Paris during the 18th century. It was their right to co-ordinate the skills of craftsmen, usually divided by the rules of their guilds, and they controlled in particular the production of items of porcelain and lacquer mounted with gilt-bronze.

69

Fig. 64
M.9 Mantel clock, gilt and patinated bronze, the figure French, 1800-25, the clock movement 1880-1920

Fig. 65
M.10 Watchstand and watch, the gilt-bronze frame, French, 1770-80, set with a Meissen figure and Sèvres flowers, the watch movement Swiss, from a London retailer

Fig. 67
M.18 Jewellery stand, gilt-brass and
mother-of-pearl, French, 1815-30

Fig. 68
M.20 Posy holder, gilt-brass and mother-of-pearl,
French, 1815-30

Fig. 66
M.14 Chamber candlestick, gilt-brass and
mother-of-pearl, French, 1815-30

M.11
Pair of Curtain Ties
French, 1815-30, possibly by Pierre-
Philippe Thomire (1751-1843) or
André-Antoine Ravrio (1759-1814)
Cast bronze, gilt and patinated
Diam: 10.8cm, 11cm
Accession nos: M.97 & a-1987

M.12
Pair of Bronze Mounts for Furniture
Italian, 1800-50
Bronze, gilded and painted
H: 9.2cm, 9.5cm W: 6cm, 5.9cm
Accession nos: M.94 & a-1987

M.13
Furniture Mount
French, 1690-1720
Gilt-bronze, pierced for a keyhole.
Identical to a mount in the Musée des Arts
Décoratifs, Paris (see Le Musée des Arts
Décoratifs: *Le Bronze*, Paris, 1910, plate
XXXIII, No. 337)
Unmarked
H:9 cm W: 14.5cm
Accession no: M.173-1987

M.14
Chamber Candlestick
French, 1815-30
Mother-of-pearl, mounted in gilt-brass
H: 6.8cm D: 12cm
Unmarked
Accession no: M.96-1987

M.15
Egg Cup
French, 1815-30
Mother-of-pearl, mounted in gilt-brass
Unmarked
H: 9.4cm Diam. of base: 9.8cm
Accession no: M.101-1987

M.16
Egg Cup
French, 1815-30
Mother-of-pearl, mounted in gilt-brass
Unmarked
H: 7.8cm Diam. of base: 9.8cm
Accession no: M.102-1987

M.17
Inkstand
French, 1815-30
Mother-of-pearl, mounted in gilt-brass
Unmarked
H: 10.7cm L: 14.1cm
Accession no: M.175-1987

M.18
Jewellery Stand
French, 1815-30
Mother-of-pearl, mounted in gilt-brass,
with hooks set round the upper tray
Unmarked
H: 14.7cm Diam. of top: 12.6cm
Diam. of base: 9.5cm
Accession no: M.100-1987

M.19
Pen Tray
French, 1830-40
Pierced and gilt-brass
The underside of the tray has been used by
an engraver as a trial plate and is covered
with arabesque doodles
H: 3.1cm L: 21.2cm W: 7.5cm
Accession no: M.104-1987

M.20
Posy Holder
French, 1815-30
Mother-of-pearl, mounted in gilt-brass
Unmarked
H: 12cm L: 12cm W: 7.8cm
Accession no: M.103-1987

M.21
Ring Stand in form of a Boat
French, 1815-30
Mother-of-pearl, mounted in gilt-brass, the
sail edges set with hooks for rings
Unmarked
H: 15cm L: 13cm W: 7.8cm
Accession no: M.98-1987

M.22
Ring Stand in form of a Boat
French, 1815-30
Mother-of-pearl, mounted in gilt-brass, the
sail edges set with hooks for rings
Unmarked
H: 14cm L: 13.7cm W: 7.1cm
Accession no: M.99-1987

Jewellery & Silver

One section of the Bequest which relates closely to Lady Abingdon herself is the group of more than fifty pieces of 20th-century jewellery and fashionable accessories. On a November day a month before her death in 1986, Mrs Hole defied her illness to welcome three curators from the V&A to see her paintings, ceramics and metalwork. She had not envisaged that the Museum would have any interest in her jewellery (largely inherited from Lady Abingdon), beyond its saleable value, but, as the jewels were unwrapped by the light of the fire, it was possible to assure her that they would splendidly enhance, and in some areas transform, the Museum's representation of work by the leading jewellery houses in London and Paris in the present century. Many of the objects are marked and have been documented with the generous assistance of colleagues in the archives of Boucheron, Cartier, Chaumet, the Garantie in Paris and Goldsmith's Hall in London.

A superb diamond and cabochon emerald brooch/pendant (M.34), forms part of the Art Deco jewellery that reflects the social eminence, supported by both aristocratic and diplomatic links, of Lord and Lady Abingdon after their marriage in 1928. From the same period are a diamond and emerald necklace convertible into two bracelets (M.35), a pin by Ostertag (M.36), and a diamond double clip brooch (M.33). The brooch can be seen in a studio photograph of Lady Abingdon (fig. 1) with the two clips separate and pointing downwards on one side of the neckline of her dress. A reaction away from platinum is represented by the lapis lazuli tassel cluster bracelet of *c.* 1937 (M.38), a relatively early example of Cartier's use of *tuyau au gaz* (gas pipe) in gold.

Contemporary with these jewels are other essentials of fashion: a Cartier cigarette case (M.62) and a vanity case made by Ramsden and Roed (M.80), both dating from 1934-5, an Ostertag silver and gold powder compact (M.79) and two wrist watches by Cartier. One of the watches was bought by the Duke of Sutherland in Paris in 1928 and may perhaps have been a wedding present to Lady Abingdon (M.72).

In the early 1960s a substantial group of objects was purchased from Boucheron in London by Lady Abingdon. They include a pair of swirling diamond, emerald, ruby and sapphire earclips with a ring, a pair of turquoise and diamond earclips with a brooch (M.48), three double rope-link necklaces, a basket-weave cigarette case (M.66) and a watch worn by Mr Hole. A large gold cigarette case made by Ramsden and Roed for Dunhill in 1960-1 records the friendship of Lord Abingdon and Mr Hole. Its lapis lazuli push recalls the Cartier bracelet of 1937 and anticipates the lapis lazuli ring (M.53) which Mr and Mrs Hole commissioned from Paul Longmire in 1985.

Lady Abingdon's jewels and accessories are the most numerous part of the precious metalwork in the Bequest, but there are fine objects from earlier periods. A silver-gilt dessert service, the knives of which were made in Lisbon, and the spoons and forks by Dehanne in Paris, reflects Stuart de Rothesay's periods of service in Portugal and France. The 5th Earl of Abingdon (1784-1854) is represented by a group of seals and his service to the town of Abingdon by an engine-turned presentation gold box of 1835-6 by A.J. Strachan. In 1876 Rose Glyn, the mother of the 8th Earl, and her sister received from Edward, Prince of Wales, two half-hoop bracelets (M. 24, M.25). Without precise provenance, but of unquestioned quality, are a slim, diamond-set, gold and platinum watch by Lacloche, of about 1910, and a shagreen-covered *étui* by Tiffany with London import marks for 1911-12. The continental crown on the *étui* suggests that it might have been a gift to the Stuart Wortleys in the years before the First World War when the guests at Highcliffe included both the King and the Kaiser.

Jewellery

M.23
Brooch
In the form of a Maltese cross with brilliant-cut diamonds, open-set in silver, backed with gold
English, *c.* 1820-40 (fitting for pin: 20th century)
Unmarked
H: 4.2cm W: 4.0cm
Accession no: M.143-1987

M.24
Half-Hoop Bangle
Gold set with half-pearls and turquoises. A glazed compartment on the inside of the hoop contains finely woven hair
English, dated 1876
Engraved 'R.R.Glyn from / H.R.H.Prince of Wales / "Serapis" 1876' (inside hoop).
Unmarked
H: 5.8cm W: 6.4cm
Accession no: M.141-1987 (fig. 69)

Edward, Prince of Wales, made a royal tour to India, 1875-6 on board H.M.S. *Serapis*. The Hon. Rose Riversdale Glyn (d.1933), daughter of Vice-Admiral Henry Carr (1829-44), A.D.C. to Queen Victoria, married Montagu Charles Francis, eldest son of the 7th Earl of Abingdon in 1885, and was the mother of Montagu, 8th Earl of Abingdon. See also M.25.

71

Fig. 69
M.24 Bangle, gold set with half pearls and turquoises, English, 1876, presented by the Prince of Wales to the Hon. Rose Riversdale Glyn

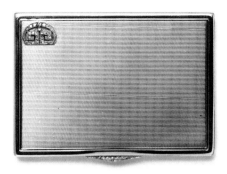

M.25
Half-Hoop Bangle
Gold set with lapis lazuli and half-pearls
Empty aperture on the inside of the hoop
would have received a glazed compartment
English, dated 1876
Engraved 'C.A. [*sic*] Glyn from / H.R.H.
Prince of Wales. / "Serapis" 1876'(inside
hoop). Unmarked
H: 5.7cm W: 6.4cm
Accession no: M.142-1987(fig.69)

The Hon. Alice Coralie Glyn (d.
unmarried 1928), was the younger sister
of Rose Riversdale Glyn and aunt of
Montagu, 8th Earl of Abingdon.
See also M.24.

M.26
Sovereign Holder
Gold-filled case containing one gold
sovereign and one half-sovereign; in the
form of a small hunter watchcase opened
by push at pendant. Coins held in place by
engine-turned spring platform
English, Birmingham, *c.*1900
Stamped 'TRADE / MARK / A.L.D / 9
CT. FILLED / 533', and with sun, moon
and star (inside case). Stamped 'GOLD-
FILLED. 9 CARAT TO WEAR 20
YEARS'
H(max.): 4.7cm Diam: 3.1cm
Accession no: M.172-b-1987

Manufactured by the watchcase company
founded in Birmingham in 1874 by A.L.
Dennison (see Philip T. Priestley, 'Watch
Case Makers of England', *NAWCC
Supplement* 20, Spring 1994).

M.27
Buckle Brooch
Rectangular, half with diamonds set in
silver and pearls, half with ebonite; backed
with gold
Western European, *c.*1900
Unmarked
L: 7.3cm W: 2.8cm
Accession no: M.126-1987

M.28
Pair of Cufflinks
Gold, vesica-shaped links. Each link has an
outer band of white enamel around green
basse taille enamel centred by a diamond
English?, *c.*1900
Marked '18CT' (on reverse of each link)
Each link: L: 1.9cm W: 0.7cm
Accession nos: M.152 & a-1987

M.29
Necklace
Four rows of cultured pearls with gold
clasp with central sapphire surrounded by
diamonds set in silver
Probably English, *c.*1900-10.
Unmarked
L: 42.8cm
Accession no: M.129-1987

M.30
Brooch
Shaped oval with diamonds set in
platinum, backed with gold
Probably English, *c.*1910-20
Engraved '18 CT / PLAT' (catch)
L: 5.6cm W: 1.6cm
Accession no: M.146-1987 (fig. 70)

M.31
Pair of Cufflinks and two matching Buttons
Platinum, set with diamonds and with
synthetic sapphires. The links and both
buttons are octagonal
English, *c.*1920
Unmarked
Each cufflink and button: L: 1.0cm W:
0.8cm
Accession nos: M.147-c-1987

Worn by Mr Hole.

M.32
Bracelet
Platinum set with diamonds. Composed of
repeated angular elements set with brilliant
and baguette-cut diamonds
Probably English, *c.*1930
Unmarked
L: 20.1cm W: 1.8cm
Accession no: M.133-1987

Fig. 70
(clockwise from top)
M.62 Cigarette case,
gold with diamonds,
London, Cartier, 1934-5

M.71 Wrist watch,
platinum with
diamonds, on a silk
strap with buckle in
gold and diamonds,
Paris, Cartier, *c.* 1930-40

M.30 Clip, platinum set
with diamonds, backed
with gold, probably
English, *c.* 1910-20

M.33
Double-Clip Brooch
Platinum set with brilliant, table and
baguette-cut diamonds
Probably English, *c.*1930
Unmarked
L: 6.0cm W: 2.7cm
Accession no: M.145-1987 (fig. 71)

In a studio photograph of Bettine, Lady
Abingdon, dating from the 1930s (fig. 1),
the clips are worn separately, with their
points facing downwards, on the neckline
of her dress. Illus: T. Hole, *Highcliffe
Castle* (privately printed, 1972), p.33.

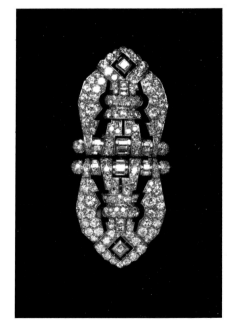

Fig. 71
M.33 Double-clip brooch, platinum set with
diamonds, probably English, *c.* 1930

M.34
Brooch / Pendant
Platinum, composed of tiers set with brilliant and baguette-cut diamonds, rising from (or descending beneath, according to use) two loops, one centred by a cabochon emerald. Another cabochon emerald is mounted at the pendant catch
French, *c.*1930
Marked on gallery: lozenge containing VP with crossed arrows, and French standard mark for platinum (dog's head, twice) L: 11.5cm W: 3.4cm
Accession no: M.140-1987 (fig. 72)

M.35
Necklace or pair of Bracelets
Platinum, composed of seven long eight-sided links, set with brilliant and baguette-cut diamonds and table-cut emeralds, alternating with links set with brilliant and table-cut diamonds and a large cabochon emerald or a table-cut diamond; white gold catch
French, *c.*1930
Restricted warranty mark for gold (eagle's head; on catch), and platinum mark (dog's head, twice; on gallery of links)
L: 38.2 cm W(max): 1.0cm
Accession no: M.139-1987 (fig. 72)

M.36
Pin
A platinum *sureté* pin in the form of a tree in a pot set with diamonds, rubies, sapphires and emerald
French, *c.*1930-40
Engraved 'OSTERTAG PARIS' (on base of pot). Restricted warranty mark for gold (eagle's head; on shaft of pin) and mixed platinum and gold mark in use from 1927 (on gallery of pot)
H: 4.5cm W: 3.3cm
Accession no: M.127-1987 (fig. 73 and back cover)

M.37
Curb-Link Bracelet
Composed of large, flattened gold links
English, 1933-4
Birmingham hallmarks for 18 ct gold for 1933-4 (on back of catch). Marked '[-]&F', perhaps for Deakin & Francis Ltd
L: 20.5cm W(max): 1.1cm
Accession no.: M.121-1987

M.38
Tassel Cluster Bracelet
Flexible gold *tuyau à gaz* strap with gold-mounted lapis lazuli beads attached by rings
French, *c.*1937

73

Fig. 73
M.36 *Sureté* pin, platinum set with diamonds, rubies, sapphires and emerald, Paris, Ostertag, *c.*1930-40

Engraved 'Cartier/04240' and with French restricted warranty marks for gold (eagle's heads three times: on catch)
L: 17.0 cm W: 3.5 cm (approx.)
Accession no: M.144-1987 (fig. 74)

Bought from Cartier, Paris, by Mr Charles Munn in 1937.

M.39
Ring
Platinum, in the form of spiral alternate rows of diamonds and emeralds, each row terminating in a square-cut diamond, the apex surmounted by an arc of baguette-cut diamonds
English, *c.*1930-40
Marked 'PLAT' and 'W.B.', oblong cameo punch with rounded ends, possibly an unregistered mark of Walter William Bouldstridge, London (marks registered in 1921 and 1929)
H: 2.5cm W: 2.0cm
Accession no: M.125-1987

M.40
Pair of Earclips
Platinum, in the form of two crossed wings of table, brilliant and baguette-cut diamonds around a central cabochon emerald set above seven table-cut emeralds
Probably English, *c.*1950
Unmarked
H: 2.5cm W: 1.8cm
Accession nos: M.117 & a-1987

Fig. 72
M.34 Brooch/pendant, platinum, diamonds, emeralds, French, *c.* 1930

M.35 Necklace or pair of bracelets, platinum, diamonds, emeralds, French, *c.* 1930

M.41
Brooch
Gold, set with diamonds. In the form of two crescents, intersecting and facing in opposed directions
English (?), *c.*1950-55
Engraved 'CHAUMET LONDON'
L: 4.9cm W(max): 2.7cm
Accession no: M.120-1987

74

M.42
Pair of Basket-Weave Cufflinks
Gold
London hallmarks for 18 ct gold for 1959-60
Engraved 'BOUCHERON' (on one part of each link). Mark of Boucheron (on both parts of each link) and marked with a crown and 18 (on links of chain). Scratched '6162' (on one link only)
Each link: 1.1cm square
Accession nos: M.151&a-1987 (fig. 76)

Bought from Boucheron, London, by Bettine, Lady Abingdon, in March 1962 for £50.

M.43
Rose-Pattern Bracelet with Tassel
Gold; a broad, coral-set ring around a thick hoop composed of twisted wire is linked by a small plain gold ring to a coral and diamond-set bell-shape from which hangs a tassel of plaited gold strands
Western European, *c.*1960
Unmarked
L.(incl. tassel): 11cm Diam: 6.6cm
Accession no: M.148-1987

M.44
Cross-over Cluster Ring
Gold, set with sapphires
Western European, *c.*1960
Mark of Robert Harry Brann Ltd (gold importer), registered 15 March 1960.
Marked '750' and '319AI.'
L: 2.6cm W: 2.2cm
Accession no: M.124-1987

M.45
Rope and Bow Bracelet
Gold, composed of seven rope double rings connected by bows
Western European, *c.*1960
London import marks for 18ct gold, perhaps 1960-1. Engraved 'Cartier' (on side of catch). Mark of Cartier, London, and stamped with 0750 in lozenge, 'LL' with star and saturn in

barrel-shaped cameo punch
L: 20.6cm W: 2.2cm
Accession no: M.134-1987 (fig. 74)

Bought from Cartier, London, on 23 August 1961.

M.46
Bracelet
Gold, in the form of a row of paired husks each set with a sapphire
English, 1960-61
London hallmarks for 18 ct gold for 1960-61
Mark of Ben Rosenfeld (Jewels) Ltd, registered 16 February 1959
L: 18.6cm W: 1.5cm
Accession no: M.135-1987

M.47
Pair of Earclips and Ring
Made of gold wire twisted into knot forms, each piece set with rows of rubies, emeralds, sapphires and diamonds, the diamonds mounted in platinum

French, *c.*1962.
Ring: stamped 'BOUCHERON' and 'MADE IN / FRANCE' and with two indistinct shields of shape used for work intended for export
H: 2.1cm W: 1.8cm
Earclips: one engraved in wrigglework 'G'
Each clip: Diam:2.3cm
Accession nos: M.118-b-1987

Bought from Boucheron, London, by Bettine, Lady Abingdon, in March 1962 for £610.

Fig. 74 (top right to bottom left)
M.53 Ring, gold set with lapis lazuli, with the crest of Bonham, London, Paul Longmire, 1985

M.38 Bracelet, gold-mounted lapis lazuli, Paris, Cartier, *c.*1937

M.45 Bracelet, gold, London, Cartier, *c.* 1960

M.81 Lipstick holder, gold engraved with the monogram of Bettine, Lady Abingdon, Paris, Cartier, 1952

Fig. 75
M.48 Pair of ear-clips and brooch, gold set with turquoises and diamonds, Paris, Boucheron, c.1963

M.48
Pair of Earclips and Brooch
Gold; each piece composed of a gold knot of crescent shapes, set with turquoises and diamonds, the latter set in platinum
French, c.1963
Engraved 'BOUCHERON MADE IN FRANCE'; stamped 'DEPOSE / SSM'; lozenge mark; obliterated French standard mark; French export marks for platinum and gold. London import marks for 18 ct gold, 1963-4
Earclips: Diam: 2.3cm
Brooch: Diam: 4.0cm
Accession nos: M.119-b-1987 (fig. 75)

Bought from Boucheron, London, by Bettine, Lady Abingdon, in November 1964 for £200 (brooch) and £214 (earclips).

M.49
Double Rope-Link Bracelet
Gold, with collet-set rubies
French, c.1963
Engraved 'BOUCHERON / MADE IN FRANCE' (under clasp). London import marks for 14 ct gold
L: 19.4cm W: 1.0cm
Accession no: M.130-1987

Bought from Boucheron, London, by Bettine, Lady Abingdon, in October 1963 for £390. See also M.50 and M.51.

M.50
Double Rope-Link Bracelet
Gold, with collet-set diamonds
French, c.1963
Engraved 'BOUCHERON / MADE IN / FRANCE' (under clasp). Incomplete London hallmarks for 18 ct gold
L: 19.5cm W: 1.0cm

In hard, blue leather box. Inscribed 'BOUCHERON / PARIS 26 Place Vendôme / New YORK, / East 57th Street, / 180, New Bond Street. / LONDON' (inside lid)
Accession no: M.131 & a-1987

Bought from Boucheron, London, by Bettine, Lady Abingdon, in October 1963 for £475. See also M.49 and M.51.

M.51
Double Rope-Link Bracelet
Gold, with collet-set sapphires
French, c.1963
Engraved 'BOUCHERON / MADE IN FRANCE' (under clasp). London import marks for 14 ct gold
L: 19.3cm W: 1.0cm
Accession no: M.132-1987

Bought from Boucheron, London, by Bettine, Lady Abingdon, in October 1963 for £375. See also M.49 and M.50.

M.52
Brooch: Sylva
Gold, set with seven sapphires. In the form of a flower, with a double pin
French, c.1967
Stamped 'CHAUMET / PARIS'. French restricted warranty mark for gold (eagle's head twice: on pin). London import marks for 18 ct gold 1968-9, with mark of Chaumet
L: 5.7cm W: 4.9cm
Accession no: M.128-1987

Brooch offered by Chaumet in 1967 in three versions: plain gold (FF 1350), gold and sapphires (FF 2450) and gold and diamonds (FF 3500).

M.53
Ring
Gold; the ring swells from the back of the hoop towards the front where the segment of lapis lazuli is engraved with a crest of a mermaid holding a mirror in her left hand
English, 1985
London hallmarks for 750 gold for 1985. Mark of Paul Longmire
H: 2.4cm W: 1.1cm
Accession no: M.123-1987 (fig. 74)

Commissioned from Paul Longmire, London, 1985. The crest is that of Bonham, the family of Mrs Hole's mother. See M.88 for a similar crest.

Boxes

M.54
Box
Circular silver box with a detachable lid and gilt interior; made from the seal of the Borough of Wallingford
Engraved on the cover with the arms of the Borough of Wallingford and inscribed 'SIGILLUM COMMUNE DE WALLINGFORD'; base engraved with the arms of the earls of Abingdon, with motto inscribed 'VIRTUS ARIETE FORTIOR' ('Virtue is stronger than the battering ram')
English, c.1710
Unmarked
Diam: 7.1cm H: 4.2cm
Accession no: M.107-1987

M.55
Box
Cartouche-shaped silver box mounted with mother-of-pearl plaques carved with scenes in low relief
Possibly German, c.1730
French restricted warranty marks in use from 1838 (on outer rim of base)
L: 8.7cm W: 1.8cm H: 6.3cm
Accession no: M.110-1987

M.56
Box
Circular, engine-turned tortoiseshell box, mounted with a gold shell and scrollwork thumbpiece. The lid mounted inside with a damaged miniature of a woman
Western European, 19th century
Indistinct marks
Diam: 7.2cm H: 3.7cm
Accession no: M.112-1987

M.57
Box
Circular tortoiseshell box with detachable lid; the top inlaid with a chevron band framing an oval of stars surrounding a crowned H
German, early 19th century
Unmarked
Diam: 5.8cm H: 2.8cm
Accession no: M.113-1987

75

M.58
Presentation Box

Rectangular gold box with an acanthus thumbpiece, engine-turned sides and base. Engraved on the outside of the lid with the arms of the corporation of Abingdon: 'PRESENTED BY / The Resident Members of the / CORPORATION OF ABINGDON / on its dissolution in December, 1835 / TO / The Rt. Honble. Montague Earl of Abingdon / High Steward of the Borough / in token of the HIGH ESTEEM they entertain for / his LORDSHIP, who has for 36 Years, shewn an / undeviating care for the Interests of the / Corporation, and the Inhabitants at large; / and in admiration of his Character as a / Nobleman, whose public worth is only excelled / by his private virtues'. Engraved on the inside of the lid beneath the arms of the Earl of Abingdon: 'WILLIAM DOE BELCHER, MAYOR / Thos..Knight, Jno..Fras..Spenlove, Jas..Cole, Chas.. King, / Jno.. V. Collingwood, Wm..Bowles Benjn.. Collingwood, / Thos..Sharps, Wm..Strange, Principal Burgesses. / Thos.. Curtis. Town Clerk,/ Richd.. Badcock. Chamberlain, / Geoe.. Bowes Morland Danl.. Godfrey, Bailiffs / Chasa.. Baster Edwd.. Cowcher, Geoe.. Shepherd, / Heny.. Dewe / Geoe.. Cox, Willm.. Tyrrel, Jno..Hyde / Thos.. Frankum. Secondary Burgesses.'
London hallmarks for 18 ct gold for 1835-6
Mark of A.J. Strachan
L: 8.0cm W: 5.7cm H: 2.2cm
Accession no: M.155-1987

Presented to Montagu, 5th Earl of Abingdon (1784-1854).

M.59
Snuff Box

Rectangular silver box engraved on the lid with Rococo scrollwork and a bearded Scottish figure wearing a kilt and holding a drawn bow, within a cartouche; interior gilt
Austrian (Vienna), 1849
Vienna marks for 13 lothig silver and 1849. Marked 'JW' (inside lid and base), probably for Josef Witek (d.1854): see W. Neuwirth, *Wiener Silber 1780-1866*, I, Vienna, 1988, p.164.
L: 8.0cm W: 4.8cm H: 1.6cm
Accession no: M.108-1987

M.60
Cigarette Case

Rectangular silver-gilt case with rounded edges. Deeply chased lines radiate from the thumbpiece
St Petersburg, *c.*1890
Marked 'J.A.'; cameo, inside rectangle with cut corners; St Petersburg mark for silver of 84 zolotniki (inside lid and base)
L: 9.1cm W: 7.8cm H: 1.7cm
In black leather slip case
Accession no: M.154 & a-1987

M.61
Box

Circular silver-gilt box with detachable lid
French, late 19th century (?)
French first standard mark for silver in use from 1838. Lozenge mark: 'A' above dog, above 'S' (outer rim of box)
D: 8.1cm H: 2.7cm
Accession no: M.109-1987

M.62
Cigarette Case

Rectangular gold case, with a pattern of parallel engraved lines within a chased line border. The lid has a double key motif in diamonds in the upper left corner. Diamond-set thumbpiece
London hallmarks for 1934-5. Mark of Cartier and London hallmarks for 9 ct gold (inside base and lid). Engraved 'Cartier London' (under thumbpiece)
L: 7.6cm W: (max): 5.3cm H: 0.9cm
In black leather slip case
Accession no: M.160 & a-1987 (fig. 70)

M.63
Cigarette Case

Rectangular gold case with horizontal ribs and ruby push. Designed to take 14 cigarettes
London hallmarks for 1958-9 (inside lid and base). Engraved 'Cartier' and 'K 8591' (rim of base). Mark of Cartier (inside base). Engraved 'The Countess of Abingdon / 2 Curzon Place, W.1.' (rim of base). Engraved, coronet and 'B' (inside of lid)
L: 8.0cm W: 6.0cm H: 1.8cm
In black leather slip case
Accession no: M.163 & a-1987

Bought from Cartier, London, on 7 August 1959.

M.64
Cigarette Lighter

Rectangular, engine-turned gilt-metal body, with a cylindrical ignition mechanism inset into one side. Engraved monogram 'B' under an earl's coronet (top of lid), for Bettine, Lady Abingdon
Swiss, *c.*1960
Stamped 'MADE IN / SWITZERLAND', 'BRIT. 726982 / USA PAT. RE 24163 / OTHERS. PENDING' and 'dunhill' (under base). Marked 'U.S.A. PAT. No. /1657352' (on mechanism)
H: 6.4cm W: 2.3cm D: 1.2cm
In hard red imitation leather fitted case, printed inside lid with royal arms and 'BY APPOINTMENT / TO HER MAJESTY THE QUEEN / SUPPLIERS OF SMOKERS' REQUISITES / ALFRED DUNHILL LTD' and 'dunhill'. With an explanatory booklet, flints and brush
Accession no: M.166 & a-1987

M.65
Cigarette Case

Rectangular, engine-turned gold case with lapis lazuli push
London hallmarks for 9 ct gold for 1960-1 (inside lid and on base). Mark of Ramsden & Roed (inside base). Engraved 'DUNHILL LONDON' (under rim of lid). Engraved 'T.R.P. HOLE, CARLTON CLUB, ST. JAMES'S STREET, LONDON, S.W.1' and with presentation inscription in facsimile handwriting 'From Montie' (inside lid)
L: 13.1cm W: 8.0cm H: 1.2cm
In brown imitation leather hard case, printed with royal arms and 'By Appointment Tobacconists / To the Late King George VI / ALFRED DUNHILL LTD' and 'dunhill' (inside lid)
Accession no.: M.165 & a-1987

Given by Montagu, 8th Earl of Abingdon, to Mr T.R.P. Hole.

M.66
Cigarette Case

Rectangular, basket-weave gold case with applied monogram of the letter E beneath an earl's coronet, for Elizabeth (Bettine), Countess of Abingdon
French, *c.*1963
Stamped 'MADE IN FRANCE', '5031', and French sponsor's mark in form used on work intended for export (on right rim

of lid). Engraved 'BOUCHERON' (on front rim of case). London 18ct/750 import marks with no date letter (on left rim of lid)
L: 7.5cm W: 5.6cm H: 1.6cm
In black leather slip case
Accession no: M.162 & a-1987 (fig. 76)

Bought from Boucheron, London, by Bettine, Lady Abingdon, in May 1963 for £300.

Watches and Desk Clocks

M.67
Desk Clock
Circular silver-gilt desk clock with pink enamel engine-turned case, white enamel dial with arabic numerals and diamond-set hands, ivory back and easel stand
French (case), 1909
Inscribed 'Cartier' (on dial). Stamped 'CARTIER' (on ivory back of case). Paris restricted warranty mark for silver (boar's head), and lozenge mark, 'E'[?]'B' (on rim of case and stand). Numbered '2660' and '.6684.' (on metal back of case) and '6684' (on easel stand)
Diam. of case: 6.2cm
Accession no: M.115-1987

Bought from Cartier, Paris, by Prince Ghika on 24 December 1909.

M.68
Desk Clock
Square desk clock with onyx and silver case inlaid with lapis lazuli; engine-turned enamelled dial with arabic numerals and blued steel hands; silvered brass easel support
Western European, c.1910
Unmarked
L: 13.5cm W: 13.5cm
Accession no: M.95-1987

M.69
Watch
Thin gold watch with platinum pendant and bow, and with edge of case set with diamonds in platinum. The dial is engine turned and silvered, with arabic numerals and blued steel Breguet hands. Associated with a chain, M.70.
French, c.1910
Inscribed 'LACLOCHE FRERES' (on dial). Engraved '43842' (on pendant). Marked: French provinces restricted

warranty mark for gold, 1838-1919 (on pendant and bow), which from April 1910 to December 1912 could also apparently be used on platinum: see 'Les Poinçons de garantie internationaux pour le platine et le palladium', p.31 in Tardy, *Les Poinçons de garantie internationaux pour l'or, le platine et palladium* (11th edition, Paris, 1984)
Diam: 4.8cm H: 6.0cm D: 0.5cm
Accession no: M.156-1987

M.70
Watch Chain
Long narrow links formed alternately of yellow gold and platinum or white gold
English, c.1910-20
Marked 'JG & S', cameo, perhaps John Goode & Sons, Birmingham, gold chain makers; indistinct caratage mark (on catch)
L: 36.5cm
Accession no: M.157-1987

M.71
Wrist Watch
Square platinum case set, on the bezel, with diamonds; silvered dial with Roman numerals. Silk strap with gold deployant buckle set with diamonds
French (case, strap), c.1930-40
Inscribed 'CARTIER' (on dial). Case: struck '1755 0483'; 'EJ' with an hour glass, the mark of Edmond Jaeger of 1, rue Vernier, 75017 Paris (mark registered 1908; see also M.72). Buckle: struck 4502; French third standard gold mark introduced in 1919 (twice); mark of Jaeger, as above (twice)
Case: L: 2.3cm W: 2.0cm
Accession no: M.137-1987 (fig. 70)

Fig. 76
M.42 Cufflinks, gold, London, Boucheron, 1959-60

M.66 Cigarette case, gold set with the monogram of Bettine, Lady Abingdon, Paris, Boucheron, c. 1963

M.72
Wrist Watch 77
Small platinum-cased watch with oblong face with arabic numerals; leather strap with platinum rings and gold deployant buckle
French (case and strap), 1928
Inscribed 'CARTIER' (on dial). Struck '04397' and with French platinum mark (dog's head, twice: on case). Struck '660', with French restricted warranty mark (eagle's head), and with mark of Edmond Jaeger, Paris (on buckle); see also M.71
Case: L: 2.5cm W: 0.6cm
Accession no: M.136-1987

Bought from Cartier, Paris, by the 5th Duke of Sutherland (d. 1963) in 1928. Possibly a gift to Elizabeth (Bettine) Stuart Wortley on the occasion of her marriage to the 8th Earl of Abingdon on 21 August 1928.

M.73
Wrist Watch
Partly gilt case with six-sided face with arabic numerals; leather strap
Swiss, perhaps c.1930
Manufactured by Gruen Watch Company. Inscribed 'GRUEN' and 'SWITZERLAND' (on dial). Stamped 'GRUEN GUILDITE BASE METAL' and scratched '42109' (on back of case). 'GRUEN' stamped (on buckle), and in raised letters (on winding piece)
L(overall): 22.6cm Case, L: 3.7cm W: 2.6cm
Accession no: M.159-1987

M.74
Wrist Watch
Lady's wristwatch with bezel of case set with diamonds. Silvered dial with blued steel hands. Silk cord strap
Swiss, c.1930-40
Dial inscribed 'MAPPIN' for Mappin & Webb, London. Marked '9 CT', oblong cameo punch (on clasp)
L(overall): 16.7cm Case, L(max.): 2.7cm W: 1.6cm
Accession no: M.149-1987

M.75

Watch

Gold square case, front and sides incised with a grid pattern; leather strap
French, *c.*1960
Stamped '.750' (on side of case). Engraved 'BOUCHERON MADE IN FRANCE / BT 1203.255' and marked incuse, the form indicating that the watch was intended for export (on back of case)
L (overall): 19.1cm Case: L:2.5cm W: 1.8cm
In brown leather hard case. Inscribed 'BOUCHERON / PARIS, 26 Place Vendôme / New YORK, / East 57th Street / 180, New Bond Street / LONDON' (inside lid)
Accession no: M.158 & a-1987

Bought from Boucheron, London, by Bettine, Lady Abingdon, in October 1963 for £85.

M.76

Wrist Watch

Gold case with square silvered dial and flexible gold bracelet
Swiss, *c.*1966
Inscribed 'JAEGER-LE-COULTRE' and 'T SWISS MADE T' (on dial). Mark on catch of De Trevers Limited, London (registered 1951); London import marks for 9 ct gold, 1966-7. Marked '375', cameo (on side of case and catch)
L(overall): 18.3cm Case, L: 1.7cm W: 1.7cm
Accession no: M.150-1987

Toilet Articles

M.77

Powder Compact

Circular silver compact with engine-turned top, base and sides. The top enamelled in yellow and with four sprays of roses around a central cross of forget-me-nots; interior gilt
Western European, *c.*1910
Unmarked. Stamped: '2' (on inside of base)
Diam: 4.9cm H: 1.2cm
Accession no: M.116-1987

M.78

Etui Containing Scent Bottle

Eight-sided shagreen-covered silver case containing a glass bottle. The body of the case is mounted with a silver crown
United States of America, *c.*1910
Engraved 'TIFFANY & Co.' (underside of base). Mark of Tiffany & Co., London hallmarks for 1910-11, London mark for imported silver, and French weevil mark for imported silver
H: 14.2cm W(max.): 7.1cm D(max.): 3.6cm
Accession no: M.111-1987

M.79

Powder Compact

Silver and gold rectangular compact decorated with bands of vertical and short horizontal lines. Twist catch set with diamonds and cabochon rubies
Paris; *c.*1930-40
Stamped 'OSTERTAG PARIS', engraved 'DÉPOSÉ 39113' and struck with limited warranty mark for silver (boars' head: on mirror frame). Marked: 'ZL' with a wheatsheaf between, for Zundel Lipec of 139 rue Ste Anne, Paris (mark registered 1928); mixed gold and silver mark (boar's head and eagle's head in an oval: inside compact)
L: 8.1cm W: 6.4cm D: 1.1cm
In black, cloth-covered slip case
Accession no: M.161&a-1987 (fig. 77)

M.80

Vanity Case

Rectangular, reeded gold vanity case, the sides enamelled in black
London, 1934-5
Mark of Ramsden and Roed (back of powder compartment). London 9 ct gold hallmarks for 1934-5 (lid and back of

powder compartment). Engraved 'W. OGDEN LTD' (retailer). Detachable lipstick marked '9' '.375'
L: 7.8cm W: 5.2cm D: 1.0cm
In black leather slip case
Accession no: M.164&a-1987

M.81

Lipstick Holder

Cylindrical, engine-turned gold and silver holder. Engraved with the crowned monogram of Bettine, Lady Abingdon
French, 1952
Engraved (on swivelling rim) 'Cartier Paris' and with punched number '01253'. Struck with cameo lozenge mark of Cartier (on cover, base and both rims). Mixed gold and silver mark (eagle's head and boar's head in oval: on both rims of base). Marked with 3rd standard gold mark (hexagon, eagle's head: on cover)
H: 5.9cm Diam.(max.): 2.3cm
Accession no: M.122-1987 (fig. 74)

Bought from Cartier, Paris, by Mme D. Thoumyre in 1952.

M.82

Lipstick Holder

Cylindrical, engine-turned gold and gilt-metal holder
London hallmarks for 9 ct gold for 1967-8. Marks of Ramsden & Roed, and London marks (on base). Contains gilt-metal and plastic holder for 'Ananda Pink' lipstick by Elizabeth Arden, London; stamped 'ELIZABETH ARDEN LONDON'
H: 5.5cm Diam: 1.9cm
In leather sheath
Accession no: M.138 & a-1987

Seals

M.83

Seal

Tall, tapering, eight-sided seal of agate in gold mounts with gold suspension bow
English, *c.*1800
Engraved with the letter 'A' beneath an earl's coronet, for an earl of Abingdon, perhaps Montagu, 5th Earl (b.1784, succeeded 1799, d.1854)
H: 3.7cm L: 2.8cm W: 2.3cm
Accession no: M.168-1987

M.84
Seal
Octagonal cornelian seal in gilt metal mounts with pierced semi-circular handle with a fixed suspension ring
English, *c.*1800
Engraved with the crest of the earls of Abingdon
H: 2.5cm L(max.): 2.1cm W: 1.8cm
Accession no: M.169-1987

M.85
Seal
Octagonal quartz seal in gold mount, the two sides of the handle formed by identical snakes, cast and engraved with suspension ring. Engraved with the arms of Bertie (Earls of Abingdon) and others impaling Gage
English, *c.*1810
Unmarked
H(excluding ring): 2.8cm L: 2.4cm
W: 2.0cm
Accession no: M.153-1987

Montagu, 5th Earl of Abingdon (1784-1854) married, as his first wife, Emily, 5th daughter of Gen. the Hon. Thomas Gage in 1807. She died in 1838. He re-married in 1841.

M.86
Seal
Oval chalcedony seal in gilt metal mounts with semi-circular handle surmounted by a fixed suspension ring
English, *c.*1810
Engraved with the arms of Montagu, 5th Earl of Abingdon (1784-1854) and with the motto 'VIRTUS ARIETE FORTIOR' ('Virtue is stronger than a battering ram')
H: 2.8cm L: 2.0cm W: 1.7cm
Accession no: M.170-1987

See preceding entry for M.85.

M.87
Seal
Rounded oblong gilt metal seal set with a cornelian. The handle is composed of two pairs of acanthus leaves scrolling upwards to a suspension loop
English, *c.*1810
Engraved with the crest of the earls of Abingdon
H: 2.1cm L: 1.4cm W: 1.2cm
Accession no: M.171-1987

M.88
Seal
In the form of an ivory hand springing from a knob decorated with naturalistic ornament. The silver-gilt seal is engraved with a mermaid holding a mirror in her left hand, and the motto 'ESSE QUAM VIDERE' ('To be rather than to seem to be')
Western European, *c.*1840-60
L: 10.3cm Diam. of knob: 2.9cm
Accession no: M.114-1987

The crest and motto are those of Bonham, the family of Mrs Hole's mother. See the ring M.53 for a similar crest.

Silver

M.89
A Pair of Ginger Jars
Silver, in baluster form with covers in Carolean style
English, 19th century
No marks
H: 27.1cm Diam: 17.3cm Weight: 1087.3 grams
a H: 26.8cm Diam: 17cm Weight: 1076.8 grams
Accession nos: M.106 & a-1987

M.90
Corkscrew
Gilt-steel worm within two silver-gilt containers of roundbox type

English, early 19th century
Engraved with monogram, 'SJBW' (on case) Unmarked
Closed, L: 6.0cm Diam.(max.): 1.2cm
Accession no: M.167-1987

M.91
Fruit or Dessert Service
Silver-gilt, comprising six forks, six spoons and six knives
Spoons and forks: Paris, 1809-19
Knives: Lisbon, early 19th century
Pointed knives with oval-section handles
Struck with a Lisbon mark, crowned 'L' within an oval (possibly that illustrated in M. Gonçalves Vidal and F. Moitinho de Almeida, *Marcas de Contrastes e Ourives Portugueses*, I Lisbon, 1974, no. 30), and an indistinct maker's mark (on blades and handles)
Forks and spoons: mark of Pierre-Joseph Dehanne (see C. Arminjon, J. Beaupuis et M. Bilimoff, *Dictionnaire des poinçons de fabricants d'ouvrages d'or et d'argent de Paris et de la Seine 1798-1838*, Paris, 1991, no. 871); Paris first standard mark and medium excise mark for silver, 1809-19.
All items engraved with the crest of Charles, Baron Stuart de Rothesay (1779-1845), including a baron's coronet (he was created Baron Stuart de Rothesay in 1828), and with the ribbon and motto of the Order of the Bath 'TRIA JUNCTA IN UNO' (he was made a Knight of the Bath in 1812)
Knives, L: 19.5cm Forks, L: 17.5cm
Spoons, L: 17.9cm
Accession nos: M.174-q-1987

Lord Stuart de Rothesay was appointed as Envoy Extraordinary and Minister Plenipotentiary to Lisbon, 1810-14, and as Envoy Extraordinary and Minister Plenipotentiary *ad interim* to Paris, June-August 1814 and Ambassador Extraordinary and Plenipotentiary to Paris, 1815-24 and 1828-31.

79

NOTES FOR PAGES 64-79

47. In the sale catalogue of 1949 these appear in different rooms as lots 13,61,62,124 and 281. This piece was not included in the sale. In each case the *chenets* were of a different pattern, but the uniting balustrades with monogram appear from descriptions (and some of the *Country Life* photos of 1942) to be identical.
48. *Un Age d'or des arts décoratifs 1814-48*, op. cit., p. 251.

49. Ernest Dumonthier, *Les bronzes du Mobilier National* (Paris: Ch. Massin, nd, *c.* 1911), pl. 26 no. 3.
50. Mary Beal and John Cornforth, op. cit., p.37.
51. In the Pontchartrain sale, Paris, December 1747, lot 133, cited, with full discussion of this model in relation to a similar pair of candlesticks in the Ashmolean Museum collections by Nicholas Penny, *Catalogue of European Sculpture in the Ashmolean Museum 1540 to the Present Day,*. vol.II (Oxford: Clarendon Press, 1992), nos 316 and 317.
52. *Catalogue des effets curieux du cabinet de feu M.*

de Selle, trésorier général de la marine, composé des tableaux....de figures et groupes de bronze....; d'ouvrage de Boulle le père et du sieur Cressent, de porcelaines anciennes...par Pierre Rémy (Paris, *chez* Didot l'ainé), 19 février 1761.
53. Nicholas Penny, op. cit., p.82.
54. Ibid. F.J.B. Watson, *Wallace Collection Catalogues. Furniture* (London: HMSO, 1956).
55. François Souchal, *French Sculptors of the 17th and 18th Centuries*, vol. I (Oxford: Cassirer, 1977), pp.191-3.

PRINTS, DRAWINGS & PAINTINGS

Fig. 78
P.1 *Giovanna of Aragon*, after
Raphael, probably 17th century

Items acquired for the Prints, Drawings & Paintings Collection were mostly related to the personalities of the Stuart, Abingdon and Hole families. A portrait by Gérard shows Lord Stuart de Rothesay during his second embassy, when plans for Highcliffe were maturing. The miniatures include work by Annie Dixon (1817-1901) and Frédéric Millet (1786-1859), each of whom painted Lady Stuart at different ages. Her daughters, Lady Canning and Lady Waterford, are also represented both as sitters and as artists. Pictures never became the prime passion of Lord Stuart de Rothesay, who was more interested in building and furnishing than in the connoisseurship of paintings, but this Bequest includes an early copy after Raphael of the portrait of *Giovanna of Aragon*, which he clearly thought much of (see p.26).

The collection was left to the Museum to be shown as the Bettine, Lady Abingdon Collection, but it is pleasing that the pictures include a portrait of Mrs Joyce Hole, our immediate benefactor. She was herself an amateur artist (grand-daughter of the Scottish artist Sir James Lawton Wingate, PRSA (1846-1924). One of her drawings (listed under her maiden name of Joyce Wingate) is also in the collection, with a handful of drawings and prints by her husband, Tahu Hole, who signed them with other elements of his name as Ronald Pearce.

Paintings

P.1
ANONYMOUS, After Raphael (1483-1520)
Portrait of Giovanna of Aragon, after the original in the Louvre; probably 17th century
Oil on canvas
115 x 92.5cm
Listed as lot 783 in the Highcliffe sale
Accession no: P.30-1987

P.2
BOUCHER, François (1703-70), in the manner of
Overdoor: *Arcadian Nymphs Making Music*; 1760-80
Oil on canvas
61 x 100cm
This can be seen in the portrait of Lord Abingdon (fig. 2)
Accession no: P.28-1987

P.3
DAVID, Antonio (born 1698), studio of
Portrait of Prince Charles Edward Stuart, 'The Young Pretender' (1720-88); 1740
Inscribed in yellow paint 'PRINCE CHA EDWARD 1740'
Oil on canvas
29.2 x 21.6cm
Listed as lot 751 in the Highcliffe sale
Probably a contemporary copy or studio version of an official half-length portrait
Accession no: P.17-1987

P.4
GERARD, François-Pascal-Simon (1770-1837)
Portrait of Lord Stuart de Rothesay; 1828-31
Inscribed 'LORD STUART-DE-ROTHESAY BY FP GERARD 1770-1837'
Oil on canvas
67.5 x 57.5cm
Accession no: P.27-1987

P.5
HURRY, Polly (Mary FARMER) (1883-1963)
Portrait of Miss Joyce Wingate (later Mrs T. R. P. Hole, 1906-1986); 1929
Signed and dated 'P. Hurry 29'
Oil on canvas
170.2 x 59.7cm
Accession no: P.20-1987

P.6
LELY, Sir Peter (1618-80)
Portrait of Ann Lee, Wife of Sir Henry Lee of Ditchley (b.1633); second half of the 17th century
Inscribed 'Ann L: y Lee, wife of Sr Henry Lee, of Ditchley in Com. Oxon Dau: of Sr Henry Danvers'
Oil on canvas
72 x 60cm
Accession no: P.18-1987

P.7
LELY, Sir Peter (1618-80)
Portrait of James Bertie (1673-1735), second son of James, 1st Earl of Abingdon; second half of the 17th century
Inscribed 'James Bertie, second son of James Earl of Abingdon'
Oil on canvas
The form of lots 742 and 768 in the Highcliffe sale suggest that this was part of a series depicting the sons of the 1st earl.
70 x 37.5cm
Accession no: P.29-1987

P.8
WATTEAU, Jean-Antoine (1684-1721), in the manner of
Figures in an Arcadian Landscape
Oil on panel
17.5 x 27.5cm
Accession no: P.25-1987

Drawings and Watercolours

P.9
ANONYMOUS: British School
View of Highcliffe and the Sea; about 1780
Pen and ink and watercolour
21.8 x 61.2cm
Accession no: P.14-1987

P.10
ANONYMOUS: British School
Napoleon Bonaparte (1769-1821); early 19th century
Verso: Studies of soldiers and a horse
Pencil and sepia wash, and (verso) pencil
26.5 x 20.9cm
Accession no: E.771-1987

P.11
ANONYMOUS: British School
Bridge over the Meuse at Namur (possibly copied from a topographical print); 1824
Inscribed in pencil on the reverse with the title and, indistinctly, 'W B Wortley[?] 1824'
Pen and ink and wash
14.2 x 20.4cm
Accession no: E.811-1987

P.12
ANONYMOUS: British School
Sketch of a landscape with trees, path and church; early 19th century
Pencil with white heightening on buff wove paper
16.6 x 24.5cm
Accession no: E.812-1987

P.13
ANONYMOUS: British School
Portrait of a man; about 1810
Inscribed 'W[?].H. Taylor'
Pencil on cream wove paper, watermarked 'J. WHATMAN 1807'
24.5 x 40cm
Accession no: E.815-1987

P.14
ANONYMOUS
Studies of a delphinium, hawk-moth and caddis fly; probably 18th century
Inscribed in white paint '15'
Watercolour on black prepared paper
27.9 x 19.7cm.
Accession no: P.19-1987

P.15
ANONYMOUS
Studies of a figure representing Abundance, with various architectural details, classical columns, a draped figure
Inscribed 'Antiscorta/ duplicat [...] ff 1 [?]'
Pen and sepia ink
33.2 x 22.5cm (irregular)
Accession no: E.805-1987

P.16
CANNING, Charlotte, Lady (1817-61)
Album of topographical views in India; March-November 1858
Watercolour, pencil, pen and ink
Volume 63.3 x 43cm, 48 pages (2 cut in half) of cream wove paper bound in boards covered with dark green cloth, quarter leather with leather ties, and marbled end-papers
Each drawing is inscribed with an identifying title and most are dated. The largest category is of general views of scenery or topographical features, e.g. 'Lower waterfall near Coonoor' (E.1160), but there are also drawings of particular buildings, e.g. 'Government House, Madras' (E.1174). There are no drawings of figures
Accession nos: E.1117-1248-1987

P.17
'Rough Sketches 1860-61', an album of topographical views in India; 1860-61
Watercolour, pencil, pen and ink and wash
Volume 63.3 x 43cm, 75 pages of cream wove paper bound in boards covered with dark green cloth, quarter leather with marbled end papers
Most are inscribed with a title and the date. The majority are landscape views, with few figure drawings or detailed studies of buildings
Accession nos: E.1249-1464-1987

P.18
HAYTER, John (1800-95)
An Old Fox Hound; 1817
Signed 'John Hayter' and dated. Inscribed in pencil with the title
Pencil and white chalk on brown-grey paper
16.9 x 14.9cm (max.)
The card mount on which the sheet is stuck down is inscribed in pencil 'Drawn in My Old Friend Edwin Landseer's Studio - 1817 - an Old Fox Hound – John Hayter'
Museum no: E. 772-1987

81

82

P.19
HELLEU, Paul Cesar (1859-1927)
Portrait of Elizabeth Stuart Wortley, later Lady Abingdon (1896-1978) and her Sister Louise (b. 1893, married Sir Percy Loraine Bt in 1924); about 1900
Coloured chalk on paper
65 x 55cm
Accession no: P.26-1987

P.20
MOSER, Mary (1744-1819)
Flowers in a vase; chrysanthemums, sunflowers, passion flowers, morning-glory and honeysuckle; 1763
Signed and dated in gouache 'Mary Moser fecit 1763'
Gouache and watercolour
57.4 x 41.2cm
Accession no: P.16-1987

P.21
Flowers in a basket; chrysanthemums, lilies, nigella, convolvulus, delphiniums; 1760s
Signed in gouache 'Mary Moser'
Gouache and watercolour
54 x 60cm
Accession no: P.22-1987

P.22
Flowers in a vase; irises, tulips, roses, forget-me-nots, delphiniums; 1767
Signed and dated in gouache 'Mary Moser fecit 1767'
Gouache and watercolour
57.4 x 41.2cm
Accession no: P.23-1987

P.23
Spring flowers in a basket; shooting-star, auricula, fritillary, columbine, tulips, hyacinths, lilies and others; 1767
Signed and dated in gouache 'Mary Moser fecit 1767'
Gouache and watercolour
54 x 60cm
Accession no: P.24-1987

P.24
MUNTZ, J. (1727-98)
Bohemian Waxwing; 1781
Signed and dated in ink 'J.H. Muntz Decemb. 1781'. Inscribed 'Ampelis Linnai Lyllema Naturae. Soitis XIII. Lanius Garrulus Linnai. in: luci Garrulus Bohemicus Gesneri Aldorrandi, Willoughi Bombicilla Bohemia – Brifson taleur de

Boheme Gallicus Leiden Schwanlagen. Germ and Turdius Polon: Jedwabniczka Jemiolucha vulgo Polon'
Pen and ink and watercolour
32 x 21.8cm
Accession no: P.15-1987

P.25
PEARCE [HOLE], [Tahu] Ronald (1908-85)
Portrait of a Woman
Verso: various sketches in pen and ink
Watercolour
76.1 x 55.5cm
Accession no: P.48-1987

P.26
Illustrations (2) to The Rubaiyat of Omar Khayyam, E.753 inscribed indistinctly in pencil on the back 'Where Destiny with' and 'Omar Khay'
Pen and ink and wash
39.4 x 29.2cm (irregular) (E.753)
32.9 x 24.4cm (irregular) (E.754)
Accession nos: E.753-4-1987
The prints after these drawings are respectively P.97 and P.98

P.27
A vulture eyeing a garden bird; on the back sketches of heads and figures, mostly humorous
Pen and ink and wash
38.2 x 28.1cm
Accession no: E.757-1987

P.28
Caricature portrait, head and shoulders of a man wearing spectacles
Signed 'Ronald Pearce'
Pen and ink and wash
23.2 x 18.8cm
Accession no: E.759-1987

P.29
An oriental in a library, with a lamp and a tiger
Signed 'Ronald Pearce'
Pen and ink and wash
38.4 x 28cm
Accession no: E.760-1987

P.30
Portrait of a man in a fantasy setting with a woman, dragon and church tower
Pen and ink and wash
39.7 x 29.2cm (irregular)
Accession no: E.762-1987

P.31
A man in a Moroccan costume, in silhouette, with an arch and a palm tree
Pencil, pen and ink and wash
38.1 x 28cm
Accession no: E.763-1987

P.32
A sheet of sketches of heads and figures, some humorous; also on the back
Pencil, pen and ink and wash, chalk, blue ball-point pen, watercolour
38.6 x 55.7cm (irregular, sheet folded in half)
Accession no: E.764-1987

P.33
The Angel of the Annunciation
Pen and ink and wash
35.6 x 25.4cm
Accession no: E.765-1987

P.34
A sheet of sketches, some humorous, of heads and figures; also on the back [includes a copy of part of Toulouse-Lautrec's drawing of 'La Goulue and Valentin le Desosse']
Inscribed in pencil 'From my window' and 'End of First Term 18 '48'
Pencil, crayon, pen and ink
56 x 38.1cm (irregular, sheet folded in half)
Accession no: E.766-1987

P.35
Sketchbook, mainly portrait studies and caricature drawings
Pencil, pen and ink and wash
Volume 31.8 x 24.3cm, 7 pages of cream wove paper bound in light brown card *c.* 1940
Accession no: E.768(1-7)-1987

P.36
WATERFORD, Louisa, Marchioness of (1818-91)
Study of a fern
Pencil and watercolour on grey paper
17.3 x 12cm
Accession no: P.49-1987

P.37
'After the fire at Tyttenhanger'
Inscribed in pencil on the mount with the title
Watercolour
15.5 x 14.9cm
Accession no: P.50-1987

P.38

Landscape with figures, houses, by a lake or river and mountains
Watercolour
10.5 x 15.1cm
Accession no: P.51-1987

P.39

Street scene with a bell tower
Watercolour
27.6 x 19.8cm (irregular)
Accession no: P.52-1987

P.40

A manor house with a tower
Watercolour
11.3 x 10.3cm
Accession no: P.52-1987

P.41

Studies of the heads of two monks in Rome
Inscribed in brown ink on the mount
'Monks. Rome'
Watercolour
16.1 x 24.2cm
Accession no: P.54-1987

P.42

A child in peasant costume holding a branch, on a country path
Inscribed with a monogram 'LSE' [?]
Watercolour
25.2 x 17.5cm
Accession no: P.55-1987

P.43

Three figures in 17th-century costume, in an interior with a dog
Watercolour
43.6 x 34.1cm
Accession no: P.56-1987

P.44

Five figures and a wounded knight in armour
Inscribed in brown ink 'Down then steppeth that fayre ladye / to help him if she maye / but when she did his beaver raise / it is my life, my Lord, she sayes / and shriekte & swoun'd away / Sir Carline'
Pen and brown ink and watercolour
32 x 44.6cm
Accession no: P.57-1987

P.45

Four figures and a dog in a noble interior
Watercolour
41.8 x 35.3cm
Accession no: P.58-1987

P.46

Two men in 17th-century costume, seated at dinner in a tavern, with a serving maid
Watercolour
53.7 x 42.3cm
Accession no: P.59-1987

P.47

Study of a flower
Watercolour
19.1 x 24.7cm (irregular)
Accession no: E.740-1987

P.48

Sketch of a young man (possibly David) holding a large sword
Pen and ink on blue paper
21.3 x 15.9cm
Accession no: E.741-1987

P.49

Sketch of a woman with a martyr's palm
Pen and ink
22.6 x 17.2cm
Accession no: E.742-1987

P.50

Woman kneeling on a cliff, a boat departing
Inscribed in pencil 'C Wortley' and in ink
'Lady L Wortley'
Pen and ink
26.2 x 31.4cm (irregular)
Accession no: E.743-1987

P.51

Sketch of a young girl with clasped hands
Black and white chalks on black paper
36.9 x 26.4cm (irregular)
Accession no: E.744-1987

P.52

Head of a woman in profile perdu; on the back a faint pencil sketch
Inscribed (twice) in pencil on the back
'Louisa'
Black crayon
25.8 x 18.8cm (irregular)
Accession no: E.745-1987

P.53

Head of a woman wearing a head-dress
Black, red and blue crayon
26.1 x 17.9cm
Accession no: E.746-1987

P.54

Head of a young man in profile, possibly from a classical sculpture, possibly Alexander
Pen and ink
23.8 x 16.5cm
Accession no: E.747-1987

P.55

Head of a woman in profile
Pen and sepia ink and wash
17.9 x 15.9cm
Accession no: E.748-1987

P.56

St John: head and shoulders
Inscribed with the title
Pen and ink
22.3 x 17.8cm (irregular)
Accession no: E.749-1987

P.57

Sketch of a curtained bed, a chair and a hand holding a bell
Pen and ink
29.1 x 23.4cm
Accession no: E.750-1987

P.58

Sketchbook with studies of figures, buildings and landscapes
Pencil, pen and ink and watercolour
Volume: 19.8 x 25.6cm. 24 pages (plus 18 cut or torn out), the cream wove paper watermarked 'GIROUX A PARIS', bound in dark-green tooled leather. With label of the retailer of the sketchbook
The sketches include a number of architectural subjects inscribed as after Prout and after Cotman's *Architectural Antiquities of Normandy* (1822). 'Granet', 'Andernach' and 'Mr Stanley' are also noted on some, perhaps indicating similar copies. Other sketches are of botanical subjects or insects
Accession no: E.774-797-1987

P.59

Boy holding a book, standing on a path
Pencil and watercolour
29.2 x 21.1cm
Accession no: E799-1987

83

P.60
Mother and child, three-quarter length, possibly after Raphael's painting of the *Madonna della Sedia*. On the back, pencil sketch of a bridge (?)
Pencil and watercolour
19.5 x 12.4cm (irregular)
Accession no: E.800-1987

P.61
'Going into the supper room'
Inscribed in ink with the title
On the back, pen sketch of two figures
Pen and ink and watercolour
22.7 x 19.3cm (irregular)
Accession no: E.801-1987

P.62
Figures in a street in Belgium (?)
Pencil
13.3 x 10.6cm (irregular)
Accession no: E.802-1987

P.63
Portrait of a woman, head and shoulders. About 1850
Pencil, black and red crayon
22.7 x 17.9cm
Accession no: E.803.1987

P.64
A woman, full length, in profile; on the back a slight pencil sketch of a woman in 18th-century dress
Pen and ink on cream wove paper
22.3 x 16.3cm
Accession no: E.808-1987

P.65
A man in 17th-century costume
Inscribed in pencil illegibly on the back
Pen and ink on cream wove paper
23.3 x 16.3cm (irregular)
Accession no: E.809-1987

P.66
Head and shoulders of a bearded man (an Apostle?); on the back a faint pencil outline of the same head
Black and white crayon on brown paper
21.9 x 16.5cm (irregular)
Accession no.: E.810-1987

P.67
A man in mid-18th-century dress
Watercolour on cream card
23.8 x 13.3cm
Accession no: E.813-1987

P.68
A woman in mid-18th-century dress
Watercolour on cream card
23.8 x 13.3cm
Accession no: E.814-1987

P.69
Album of sketches and studies; about 1833-9
Pen and ink and wash, pencil, watercolour
Volume 44.6 x 28.3cm. 81 pages (some missing, one cut) of alternate buff, cream and brown wove paper, bound in boards covered in marbled paper and quarter leather
The collection includes studies of men, women and children, sometimes in historic costume, in interiors and other picturesque settings; some suggest particular countries, including Spain; a few are of Biblical subjects, some after famous paintings. E.929-930 and E.937 possibly depict the singer Pasta, who sang the premiere of Bellini's *Norma* in London in 1833
Accession no: E.816-945-1987

P.70
Album of drawings; about 1832-4
Pencil, chalks, pen and ink and wash, watercolour
Volume 39.3 x 47.7cm. 24 pages, 3 cut and several cut out, bound in boards covered in marble paper and quarter leather, with marbled end papers
The collection includes many portraits, some with dates and inscriptions identifying the sitters, or adding notes on the sources of study drawings after famous paintings
Accession nos: E.946-1036-1987

P.71
'Rough Sketches 1854-5', an album of landscape drawings
Variously inscribed
Pencil, pen and ink and wash, watercolour
Volume 64 x 43.3cm. 43 pages of wove cream paper, plus several cut out, bound in boards covered in dark green leather with leather ties, embossed in gold with the title
The collection includes views and details of ornament, and some interiors and copies of pictures at Wilton, Broadlands, Highcliffe, Hurst Castle, Panshanger, Tyttenhanger, Whippingham, Windsor, Osborne, Albury, Aldenham, Buildwas Abbey, Appley and picturesque sites in Ireland and Scotland, including Balmoral; overseas sites identified include several in Norway and Hamburg
Accession nos: E.1037-1116-1987

P.72
Profile portrait of a woman. 1836
Inscribed in brown ink 'LS. Fribourg. Sept. 26 1836'
Pencil and watercolour
28.5 x 24cm (irregular)
Accession no: E.1473-1987

P.73
Portrait of a young woman
Pencil and watercolour
27.8 x 18.8cm (irregular)
Accession no: E.1474-1987

P.74
Study of a girl kneeling at prayer; sketch of a girl's head on the back
Pencil and watercolour
27.5 x 18.7cm (irregular)
Accession no: E.1475-1987

P.75
Sketch of a woman with a baby and two children
Pencil and watercolour
28.7 x 20.9cm (irregular)
Accession no: E.1476-1987

P.76
Three women and a child in 17th-century costume, in an interior; on the back a sketch of two seated women
Inscribed 'Honi soit qui mal y pense'
Pen and ink and watercolour
19.1 x 23.5cm (irregular)
Accession no: E. 1477-1987

P.77
Landscape with mountains and a lake
Pencil and watercolour
25.7 x 35.2cm
Accession no: E.1478-1987

P.78
WINGATE, Joyce M. (Mrs T.R.P. Hole) (1906-86)
A tethered lion surrounded by black mice
Inscribed in ink on the back by 'J.M. Wingate 20 Grove Court N.W.8 if rejected, please return to this address'; before 1929
Pen and ink
39.4 x 29.1cm (irregular)
Possibly an illustration to Aesop's fable of the lion destined to fight in the Roman arena but rescued by mice, who chewed through the ropes that tethered him.
Accession no: E.758-1987

84

Fig. 79
P.84 Miniature, thought to be of Philip, 3rd Earl of
Hardwicke, about 1820

Fig. 80
P.85 Miniature thought to be of Viscount Eastnor
and his wife, about 1820

P.79
**YORKE, Lady Elizabeth Margaret, later
Lady Stuart de Rothesay (1789-1867)**
Sketchbook, mostly landscapes and studies
of architecture in Holland, Belgium,
France and Germany
Inscribed in ink on the frontispiece
'ELIZABETH YORKE August. 1814'
Pencil, pen, ink and sepia and blue wash
Volume 14.7 x 20.1cm. 35 pages of cream
wove paper bound in boards covered in
gold-tooled brown leather, stamped 'Smith
Walker & Co. 9 & 11 Piccadilly'
Accession no: E.798-1987

P.80
A woman in court dress
Inscribed in pencil 'June [?] 17. 1816'
Pencil and wash
23 x 18.4cm (irregular)
This sheet seems to have been torn from a
sketchbook. The drawing may record an
occasion at the court of Louis XVIII
Accession no: E.804-1987

P.81
**Studies (3 on 2 sheets) of a seated young
woman reading; about 1805-15**
Pencil
28.6 x 43.6cm (irregular): E.806
28.2 x 43.3cm (irregular): E.807
Museum nos: E.806-807-1987

Miniatures

P.82
ANONYMOUS: British School
Marchioness of Waterford (1818-91); about
1840-50
Watercolour and ivory mounted on card;
framed with P.86
91 x 70mm
The identification of P.86 as Lady Canning
suggests that this is her sister, possibly a
copy of a professional piece by a member
of the family
Accession no: P.21-1987

P.83
**ANONYMOUS, after Sir W.C. Ross RA
(1794-1860)**
Viscountess Canning (1817-61); about
1840-50
Watercolour and ivory mounted on card
146 x 110mm
The identification is after a mezzotint by
J. Thomson, 1843, in the Archive of the
National Portrait Gallery. The copy may
be by a family member
Accession no: P.31-1987

P.84
ANONYMOUS: British School
Unknown man wearing the Order of the
Garter, possibly Philip, 3rd Earl of
Hardwicke, K.G. (1757-1834), the father
of Lady Stuart de Rothesay; about 1820
Inscribed in ink on backboard 'Lady
Stuart de Rothesay'
Watercolour and ivory mounted on card
132 x 108mm
Accession no: P.32-1987

P.85
ANONYMOUS: British School
Unknown man and woman in Van Dyke
costume, with a dog, possibly Viscount
and Viscountess Eastnor (later Earl and
Countess Somers), the sister and brother-
in-law of Lady Stuart de Rothesay; about
1820
Inscribed in ink on backboard 'Lady
Stuart de Rothesay'
Watercolour on ivory mounted on
pasteboard
133 x 106mm
Accession no: P.34-1987

P.86
ANONYMOUS, after Sir W.C. Ross RA (1794-1860)
Viscountess Canning (1817-61); about 1840-50
Watercolour on ivory; framed with P.82
90 x 71mm
Accession no: P.37-1987

P.87
MILLET, Frédéric (1786-1859)
Elizabeth, Lady Stuart de Rothesay (1789-1867); 1819
Signed and dated indistinctly
Watercolour, partially backed with silver leaf, on ivory mounted on pasteboard
142 x 106mm
The identification is from a mezzotint by W. Giller, published in *La Belle Assemblée* for November 1827 (new series), no. 35
Accession no: P.33-1987

P.88
DIXON, Annie (1817-1901)
Elizabeth, Lady Stuart de Rothesay (1789-1867); 1865
Inscribed on the backing card 'Lady Stuart de Rothesay / Painted by A. Dixon 1865'
Watercolour on ivory mounted on card
86 x 76mm
Accession no: P.36-1987
Illus.: A.J.C. Hare *The Story of Two Noble Lives* (1892), vol.III, p.42

86

Fig. 81
P.87 Miniature of *Elizabeth, Lady Stuart* (later Lady Stuart de Rothesay), by Frédéric Millet, 1819

Fig. 82
P.88 Miniature of *Elizabeth, Lady Stuart de Rothesay*, by Annie Dixon, 1865

P.89
THORSBURN, Robert (1818-85)
Henry, 3rd Marquess of Waterford, in armour as the 'Knight of the Dragon' at the Eglinton Tournament; 1840
Typewritten label on the back lettered 'Henry de la Poer, 3rd Marquess of Waterford 1811-1859. Painted 1840'
Watercolour on ivory
112 x 85mm
Accession no: P.35-1987
Illus.: A.J.C. Hare, *The Story of Two Noble Lives* (1892), vol. I, p.228

Prints

P.90
BEARDSLEY, Aubrey Vincent (1872-98), after
Plate 54 to H.C. Marillier *The Early Work of Aubrey Beardsley* (John Lane, the Bodley Head, London), 1899. The Comedy Ballet of Marionettes, I from *The Yellow Book*, vol. II, July 1894, following p.85
Line block
17 x 12.3cm
Accession no: E.751-1987

P.91
Plate 96 to *The Later Work of Aubrey Beardsley* (John Lane, The Bodley Head, London), 1901. The Billet-Doux, headpiece of the first canto of *The Rape of the Lock* by Alexander Pope, published by Leonard Smithers, London, 1896
Line block
11 x 10.8cm
Accession no: E.752-1987

Fig. 83
P.89 Miniature of *Henry, 3rd Marquess of Waterford* by Robert Thorsburn, 1840

P.92
**GEOFFROY, Charles Michel (1819-82)
and DIAZ DE LA PENA, Narcisse
Virgile (1808-76)**
La Lecture du Roman
French, 1840-60
Lettered 'Diaz pinx:/Geoffroy sc.'
Numbered '9'. With an oblong blind
stamp lettered 'LES PEINTRES
VIVANTS'
Etching, engraving, stipple engraving,
roulette work and machine ruling, India
proof
40.7 x 29.2cm
Accession no: E.761-1987

P.93
HAYES, William (1735-1802)
American blue finch; 1777
Inscribed with the title, signed in ink
'Hayes' and dated 1777
Etching coloured by hand
Cut to 25 x 17.5 cm
Accession no: E.769-1987

P.94
HAYES, William (1735-1802)
Red macaw; 1777
Inscribed with the title, signed in ink 'W
Hayes' and dated 1777
Etching, coloured by hand
Cut to 55 x 38.2cm
Accession no: E.770-1987

P.95
**KIP, Johannes (1653-1722) and KNYFF,
Leonard (1650-1722)**
'Wythame in the County of Berks one of
the Seats of the Rt Honble Montague Earle
of Abingdon, Baron Norreys of Rycott
Within two Miles of Oxford'. Plate from
vol. I of *Nouveau Theatre de la Grande
Bretagne*, published by David Mortier,
London, 1715. With armorial shield
Lettered with the title and 'L. Knyff Del.'
and 'I.Kip Sc.'; with armorial shield;
numbered 35
35.6 x 49.1cm
Accession no: E.1472-1987

P.96
MANET, Edouard (1832-1883)
Le Chanteur Espagnol; 1862
Signed 'ed Manet'; inscribed 'imp Delatre
Paris'
Etching and retroussage
29.7 x 24.4cm
Accession no: E.1471-1987

P.97
**PEARCE [HOLE], [Tahu] Ronald (1908-
85)**
Cowled figure in a hallway. Illustration
[unpublished] to *The Rubaiyat of Omar
Khayyam* by Edward Fitzgerald, first
published London, 1859
Line block
Size of sheet 37.9 x 25.5cm
The drawing by the artist after which this
print was made is E.753-1987 (P.26)
Accession no: E.755-1987**P.98**

P.98
**Half length of an oriental man against a
landscape background.** Illustration
[unpublished] to *The Rubaiyat of Omar
Khayyam* by Edward Fitzgerald, first
published London, 1859
Line block
Size of sheet 34.4 x 28.8cm
The drawing by the artist after which this
print was made is E.754-1987 (P.26)
Accession no: E.756-1987

P.99
PICASSO, Pablo Ruiz (1881-1973)
*Cephale tue par megarde sa Femme
Procris*; 1930
Illustration from a set of 30 for *Les
Metamorphoses d'Oude* translated into the
French by Georges Le Faye. Printed by
Louis Fort. Published by Albert Skira,
Lausanne, 1931
Etching
31.4 x 22.4cm
Accession no: E.1470-1987

**P.100 REMBRANDT HARMENSZ
VAN RYN (1606-69) and
BRETHERTON, James (fl. 1770-c.1790)
Beggar seated on a bank**
Copy by James Bretherton
Signed and dated 'RHL [monogram] 1630'
Inscribed in ink on the back 'F.D. 1843'
Etching
11.5 x 6.9cm
Accession no: E.773-1987

87

The ceramics from the Bequest almost certainly derive from the original collections at Highcliffe, though the sale catalogue of 1949 lists almost no Sèvres apart from a large white and gold service (lots 220 and 221). By the 1820s the trade in *vieux Sèvres* to English collectors was flourishing both in France and in England. There is no specific mention of the collecting of porcelain in Lord Stuart's letters and it is possible, on the evidence of the porcelain-mounted cabinets (F.19), that this was Lady Stuart's taste. Certainly, the workbox (C.16), which is likely to have been hers, relates to the Palais Royal pieces (M.14-M.22), which may represent the shopping tastes of Lady Stuart de Rothesay. The Paris porcelain dessert dish and its Derby copy illustrate a utilitarian rather than a collector's view of more recent French porcelain. Clearly this was the domestic kit that went with an Empire interior, and when the whole was translated to England it became necessary to allow for replacements. We can see Lady Stuart concerning herself with both old and new Sèvres in letters of the 1840s referred to in the essay (p. 35). A single piece of French 20th-century glass was bequeathed, presumably a piece acquired by Lady Abingdon herself.

C.1
Cup and Saucer *(Gobelet calabre)*
French (Vincennes); about 1752
Soft paste porcelain painted in enamel colours and gilded, with exotic birds in reserves against a dark blue ground *(bleu lapis nuagé)*
Marks: Cup: interlaced Ls in underglaze blue, '3' incised. Saucer: 'o' incised
H: 7.4cm Diam: 7.2cm Diam. of saucer: 13.8cm
Accession nos: C.255 & a-1987 (fig. 84)

C.2
Teapot and Lid *(Theière calabre)*
French (Sèvres); 1764
Soft past porcelain, painted in blue enamel with flowers
Marks: Interlaced Ls enclosing 'L' in blue enamel
H: 11.4cm Diam: 11cm L: 18.2cm
H with lid: 13.9cm
Accession nos: C.240 & a-1987 (fig. 84)

C.3
Cup and Saucer *(Tasse à l'anglais)*
French (Sèvres); 1765
Cup of soft paste, saucer of hard paste, painted in enamel colours with landscapes in reserves on a purple ground and gilded
Marks: Interlaced Ls enclosing 'm' and and

Fig. 84 (left to right)
C.11 Cup and saucer, Sèvres, *c.* 1790, hard paste porcelain, painted in enamel colours and gilded

C.1 Cup and saucer, Vincennes, *c.* 1752, soft paste porcelain, painted in enamel colours and gilded

C.2 Teapot and lid, Sèvres, 1764, soft paste porcelain, painted in blue enamel

C.3 Cup and saucer, Sèvres, 1765, cup of soft paste and saucer of hard paste, painted with enamels and gilded

axe, the mark of the painter Rosset (fl. 1753-95), in blue enamel. Cup: '41' and '17' incised. Saucer: '42' incised
H: 4.8cm Diam: 8.5cm Diam. of saucer: 13.5cm
Accession nos: C.252 & a-1987 (fig. 84)

C.4
Two-handled Cup and Saucer *(Gobelet à lait)*
French (Sèvres); 1767
Soft paste porcelain, painted in enamel colours with fan motifs and gilded
Marks: Interlaced Ls enclosing 'O' in blue enamel. Cup 'tb' and '&' incised. Saucer '&' incised
H: 8.9cm Diam: 9.8cm Diam. of saucer: 19cm
Accession nos: C.236 & a-1987 (fig. 85)

Fig. 85
C.4 Two-handled cup and saucer, Sèvres, 1767, soft
paste porcelain, painted in enamel colours and gilded

C.9 Covered cup and cover, Sèvres, 1784, soft paste
porcelain, painted in enamel colours and gilded

C.5 Two-handled cup and saucer, Sèvres, c. 1769,
soft paste porcelain, painted in enamel colours
and gilded

C.5
Two-handled Cup and Saucer *(Gobelet à lait)*
French (Sèvres); about 1769
Soft paste porcelain, painted in enamel colours with flowers within trellised panels and gilded
Marks: Cup and saucer: 'S' backwards incised. Saucer: Interlaced Ls and 'LG', the mark of Le Guay *père*, painter (fl. 1749-96), in blue enamel
H: 8.9cm Diam: 9.7cm Diam. of saucer: 18.7cm
Accession nos: C.245-b-1987 (fig. 85)

C.6
Half-size Wine Bottle Cooler *(Seaux à demi-bouteille)*
French (Sèvres); 1770-80
Soft paste porcelain, painted in enamel colours with sprays of flowers and gilded
Marks: Interlaced Ls, partially obliterated. An axe in blue enamel, the mark of the painter Rosset (fl.1753-95). 'LB' and 'ch' incised
H: 16.8cm Diam: 18.1cm
Accession no: C.244-1987

C.7
Tureen and Cover *(Pot à oille)*
French (Sèvres); 1770-80
Soft paste porcelain with applied prunus sprays, painted in enamel colours with flowers and gilded
Marks: Interlaced Ls in blue enamel
H: 24.5cm Diam: 24.7cm
Accession nos: C.256 & a-1987 (fig. 86)

C.8
Ice Pail, Liner and Cover *(Seau à glace)*
French (Sèvres); 1778
Soft paste porcelain, painted in enamel colours with sprays of flowers and gilded
Marks: Interlaced Ls enclosing 'AA', and 'BD', the mark of Baudouin *père* the gilder and 'L' in blue enamel, the mark of Denis Levé (fl.1754-c.1800)
H: 12.4cm, with lid: 20.8cm Diam: 19.4cm
Accession nos: C.237-b-1987 (fig. 86)

C.9
Covered Cup and Saucer *(Tasse enfoncée et trembleuse)*
French (Sèvres); 1784
Soft paste porcelain painted with enamel

colours with landscapes within reserves (including a ballooning scene) and gilded
Marks: Interlaced Ls with 'gg' and a label of three points, the mark of the painter Vieillard (fl. 1753-90), all in purple enamel. Cup: '37a' over '9' incised. Saucer: '36' incised
H: 8.6cm Diam: 8.2cm Diam. of saucer: 15cm
The handle is a replacement
Accession nos: C.246-b-1987 (fig. 85)

C.10
Cup and Saucer *(Gobelet litron)*
French (Sèvres); about 1790
Hard paste porcelain, moulded decoration, painted in enamel colours and gilded with chinoiseries in reserves against a black ground
Marks: Cup: 'CD' 'rn' '18 incised. Saucer: 'BY' [DY?], 'rn' incised; black dot on the rim
H: 6.8cm Diam: 6.2cm Diam. of saucer: 14.1cm
Accession nos: C.253 & a-1987

C.11
Cup and Saucer *(Gobelet litron)*
French (Sèvres); about 1790
Hard paste porcelain painted in enamel colours and gilded with chinoiseries in imitation of *cloisonné* enamels within 'cloud-shaped' reserves on a purple ground
Marks: Interlaced Ls with a crown above and the mark of Dieu (fl.1777-1811) in red enamel
H: 6cm Diam: 5.9cm Diam. of saucer: 12.8cm
Accession nos: C.254 & a-1987 (fig. 84)

Fig. 86
C.7 Tureen and cover, Sèvres, 1770-80, soft paste porcelain with applied decoration painted in enamel colours and gilded

C.8 Ice pail and cover, Sèvres, 1778, soft paste porcelain painted in enamel colours and gilded

Fig. 87
C.13 Dessert dish, possibly La Courtille, 1800-20, hard paste, moulded and painted with enamel and gilded

C.14 Dessert dish, Derby, c.1825-30, soft paste, moulded and painted with enamel colours and gilded

C.12
Soup Plate, Octagonal
French (made at Creil et Montereau, printed by Stone, Coquerel and Legros); about 1815
Cream-coloured earthenware, transfer printed in greenish brown with a landscape scene, lettered below 'CHATEAU DE HIGH CLIFF, Comté d'Hamps Angleterre', with moulded beading to the rim
Marks: Impressed CREIL and printed '26', and 'SCL' in monogram encircled by 'PAR BREVET D'INVENTION...PARIS'
W across corners: 24.8cm
Accession no: C.239-1987 (fig. 9)

C.13
Dessert Dish in the shape of a Shell
French (Paris, possibly La Courtille); 1800-20
Hard paste porcelain, moulded and painted with enamel colours and gilded
Marks: Imitation crossed swords with a circle in the middle, in underglaze blue (untraced); one further (unreadable) mark
W: 24.7cm
Accession no: C.250-1987 (fig. 87)

Fig. 89
C.16 Label of the retailer, Feuillet

C.14
Dessert Dish in the shape of a Shell
English (Derby); about 1825-30
Soft paste porcelain, moulded and painted with enamel colours and gilded
Marks: Gothic 'D' surmounted by an angular crown, painted in red
W: 24cm
Probably made as a replacement to match the Paris dish, which is slightly earlier in date
Accession no: C.251-1987 (fig. 87)

C.15
Ink Stand
French (Paris); about 1820-30
Hard paste porcelain painted in enamel colours with a frieze of flowers and gilded; mounted in ormolu
Unmarked
H: 16.5cm
Accession No: C.259-1987

C.16
Workbox
French (Paris, the porcelain probably by Darte Frères, rue de Charonne, the box assembled and sold by Feuillet); about 1820
Porcelain mounted in gilt-bronze, the panels painted in enamel colours with flowers and butterflies, in reference to Psyche, and gilded; the workbox is lined with silk. Marks: Painted on porcelain interior 'Feuillet Rue de la paix 18'. Paper label on the base reads 'Rue de la Paix No. 18 / entre la place Vendôme et le Boulevard / Feuillet / Fabricant et Peintre sur Porcelaines / Bréveté de S.A.S. Mgr. le Prince de Condé / et de S.A.S. Mgr le Duc de Bourbon / Tient Magasn. de Porcelaines /et Cristaux / A Paris'
H: 13.7cm L: 25.2cm
Accession no: C.260-1987 (figs 88 and 89)

Fig. 88
C.16 Workbox, the porcelain possibly by Darte Frères, mounted in gilt-bronze and sold by Feuillet, rue de la paix, Paris, c. 1820

Fig. 90
C.17 Basket, Meissen, 1740-60, hard paste porcelain, moulded and pierced, painted in enamel and gilded

C.24 Basket, Worcester, probably decorated in the London workshop of James Giles, 1770-75, soft paste porcelain with moulded and applied ornament, painted in underglaze blue and enamels and gilded

C.18 One of a pair of baskets, Meissen, 1740-60, hard paste porcelain, moulded and pierced, painted in blue enamel and gilded

C.17
Basket
Germany (Meissen); 1740-60
Hard paste porcelain with piercing and applied, moulded decoration, painted in enamel, and gilded
Marks: Crossed swords in underglaze blue
L: 25.5cm
Possibly *en suite* with C.18 (C.248&a-1987)
Accession no: C.247-1987 (fig. 90)

C.18
Pair of Baskets
Germany (Meissen); 1740-60
Hard paste porcelain with piercing and applied, moulded decoration painted in blue enamel, and gilded
Marks: Crossed swords in underglaze blue
Diam: 17.7cm
Possibly en suite with C.17 (C.247-1987)
Accession Nos: C.248 & a-1987 (fig. 90)

C.19
Snuff Box, a flattened Barrel with two Compartments
Germany (Meissen); 1740-60 ?
Hard paste porcelain with moulded decoration, painted in enamel colours with flower sprays, the interior of one lid with a hunting scene ; one lid of hardstone or glass (replaced); mounted in copper gilt,
the interiors gilded
Unmarked
H: 8cm
Accession no: C.249-1987 (fig. 91)

C.20
Bowl
Germany (Meissen); 1745-50
Hard paste porcelain, moulded and painted in enamels with flower sprays and gilded
Marks: Crossed swords in underglaze blue
Diam: 23.2cm
Accession no: C.242-1987 (fig. 92)

C.21
Teapot and Lid
Germany (Meissen); 1750-60
Hard paste porcelain, moulded and painted in enamels with landscapes and Rococo cartouches and gilding
Marks: Crossed swords in underglaze blue
H: 10cm
Accession nos: C.241 & a-1987 (fig. 91)

Fig. 91
C.21 Teapot, Meissen, 1750-60, hard paste porcelain, moulded and painted in enamels and gilded

C.19 Snuff-box, Meissen, 1740-60 (?), hard paste porcelain, moulded, painted in enamels and gilded, mounted in copper gilt

Fig. 92
C.22 Tureen and cover, Meissen, 1763-74, hard paste porcelain, moulded, painted with enamel colours and gilded

C.20 Bowl, Meissen, 1745-50, hard paste porcelain, moulded and painted in enamels and gilded

C.22
Tureen and Cover
German (Meissen); 1763-74
Hard paste porcelain, with moulded borders and knop, painted in enamel colours with floral sprays and gilded
Marks: Crossed swords and dot in underglaze blue
H: 16.2cm L: 20cm
Accession nos: C.235 & a-1987 (fig. 92)

C.23
Tureen, Cover and Stand
Italian (Doccia); about 1780
Hard paste porcelain, moulded and painted in enamel colours and gilded, the glaze whitened with tin oxide
Marks: A star painted in red
H: 12.2cm Diam: 23cm
Accession nos: C.257-b-1987 (fig. 93)

C.24
Basket
English (Worcester, probably decorated in the London studio of James Giles (1718-80)); 1770-75
Soft paste porcelain, with moulded and applied ornament, painted in underglaze blue and enamel colours with urns and flowers and gilded
Marks: A crescent painted in underglaze blue
L: 21.7cm
Accession no: C.243-1987 (fig. 90)

C.25
Figure of a Lion Couchant
English (Derbyshire, probably Brampton); 1840-60
Salt-glazed brown stoneware, press-moulded
Unmarked
L: 15.5cm
Accession no: C.238-1987

C.26
Vase
French (Marcel Goupy); about 1925
Glass, hand-blown, decorated with coloured enamels and gilding
Marks: 'M. Goupy' painted in enamel
H: 18cm D: 18.5cm
Accession no: C.258-1987

Fig. 93
C.23 Tureen, cover and stand, Doccia, *c.* 1780, hard paste porcelain, moulded and painted in enamels and gilded

SCULPTURE

Fig. 95
S.2 Plaster cast of
heroic head, British,
*c.*1880-1910, supplied
by D. Brucciani after a
Classical original in the
British Museum

S.1

Wax Relief of Louis XVI, mounted on a box
French, 1804-9
Wax relief of the King shown in profile, against ebony, the box of tortoiseshell and ebony with gold mounts surrounding the domed glass
Struck on the lid with the mark of Benoit Rondoni of Paris (registered 1804-5; C. Arminjon *et al.*, *Dictionnaire des poinçons de fabricants d'ouvrages d'or et d'argent de Paris et de la Seine, 1798-1838* (Paris, 1991), no. 00536), and on the base with the third standard mark for gold, 1798-1809, and the *moyenne garantie* mark, 1798-1809. The gold lining to the lid is a replacement: it bears the mark of Catherine-Adelaïde Duponnois of Paris (registered 1822; *ibid.*, no. 00886), and the 3rd standard gold mark for 1819-38
H: 2.2cm Diam: 8.1cm
Accession nos: A.2&a-1987

S.2

Heroic Head
English, about 1880-1910
D. Brucciani, after a head in the British Museum, a Roman copy of a Classical or early Hellenistic original, possibly depicting Hermes of Lysippus, found at Ostia *c.* 1795 (inv. no. GR 1856.5-12.8). The cast appears in the catalogue of D. Brucciani & Co. (1892) no. 2258
Plaster
Impressed on the back 'D BRUCCIANI'
H: 54cm approx.
Accession no: A.3-1987

Fig. 94
S.1 Wax relief of Louis
XVI, mounted on a
box, French, 1804-9

TEXTILES & DRESS

T.1
Fragment, from a set of Bed Hangings
French, c.1775-90
Cream satin embroidered with silks and
chenille, part of a set of hangings said to
have belonged to Queen Marie Antoinette.
Exhib: *Marie Antoinette, Archiduchesse,
Dauphine et Reine*, Versailles, 1955, no.
723
H: 68.6cm W: 156.2cm
Accession no: T.56-1987

T.2
Carpet or Hanging *(Portière)*
French (Aubusson), *c.*1840-80
Wool. Warp count 13 to the inch
Woven with the arms of a continental
baron, gules, on a bend argent 3 crosses
gules (unidentified)
L: 236.2cm W: 202.5cm
Accession no: T.59-1987

T.3
Cushion Cover
English or Welsh, 1930-40
Satin, with quilted decoration
L and W: 64.1cm
Accession no: T.57-1987

T.4
Cushion Cover
English or Welsh, 1930-40
Taffeta, with quilted decoration
L: 90.8cm W: 82.5cm (including frill)
Accession no: T.57a-1987

T.5
Two Table Napkins
English, 1880-1900
White linen damask, with hand-worked
picot edging
Marked in ink 'SW' (possibly for Stuart
Wortley) and embroidered in yellow yarn
'54'
L and W: 30.5cm
Accession no: T.63 & a-1987

T.6
Fan
French?, the sticks and guards 1700-25, the
leaf *c.* 1790
Double paper leaf, painted, gilded and
embroidered with sequins; sticks and
guards of carved ivory with mother-of-
pearl inlay and *piqué* decoration
H: 28cm W: 40.6cm
Accession no: T.61-1987

T.7
Fan
French, 1850-60
Double paper leaf, printed with
lithograph, possibly of Aurora in her
chariot, with painted and printed
decoration; sticks and guards of bone
H: 24.2cm W: 45.8cm
Accession no: T.62-1987

T.8
Cane
English, 1919, made for the 8th Earl of
Abingdon
Mahogany, the knob of tiger's-eye agate,
collared in gold
Collar engraved 'LORD NORREYS
CARLTON CLUB' and, in smaller letters,
'BENCOX/LONDON'. Struck with the
leopard's head, the date letter for 1919, the
carat mark '12.5' and the mark 'JC',
possibly for John Robert Cooke, stick
mounters
L: 91cm
Accession no: T.60-1987

T.9
Jacket
French, Jean Patou, 1950-60
White fur, with bell sleeves; lining of
cream silk
Label: 'Jean Patou/ Paris'
L: 42cm W at shoulders: 42cm
Accession no: T.58-1987

BOOKS & MANUSCRIPTS

The importance of books to Lord Stuart de Rothesay is discussed in the essay on his collecting (pp. 25-6). His immense library was sold in London in 1855, the sale conducted by Messrs S. Leigh, Sotheby and John Wilkinson and lasting 15 days.[1] Clearly not everything was sold and some books must have remained with the family. These books represent many of Lord Stuart de Rothesay's interests in travel, literature, fine printing and family history. Heraldry was also a passion and is reflected in five different armorial stamps found on these books. Though it is not possible to date these variant stamps, they are offered in what we hope is the correct chronological order (figs 96-100). The majority of the books in the Bettine, Lady Abingdon Collection are from Lord Stuart de Rothesay's library, but a few later books were also accepted as useful additions to the National Art Library.

From the Library of Lord Stuart de Rothesay

(See figs 96-100 for the various Stuart armorial plates)

Almanach des modes. **Paris: Chez Rosa, 1814.**
Stuart arms version 2

Almanach para o anno de 1798. **Lisbon: Typog. da Academia Real, 1798.**
Portuguese royal arms. Ink inscription 'Honbl. Genl. Stuart'

Almanak mercantil ó Guia de comerciantes para el año de 1808. **Madrid: Vega, 1808.**
Stuart arms version 3

AUDIFFRED, Hyacinthe
Un mois à Vichy: guide pittoresque.
Paris: Dauvin & Fontaine, 1849
Ink inscription 'E. Stuart de Rothesay'

BARTHEZ, François
Guide pratique des malades aux eaux de Vichy, precedé de l'histoire et de la topographie de Vichy et de ses environs.
Paris: J.-B. Baillisere, 1849
BERNIS, François-Joachim de Pierre de
Correspondence du Cardinal de Bernis, ministre d'état, avec M. Paris-du-Verney,

conseiller d'état, depuis 1752 jusqu'en 1796. London: Et se trouve à Paris chez Cuchet, 1790. 2 vols
Stuart arms version 1

BRUNEL, Antoine de, *et al.*
Voyage d'Espagne: contenant entre plusieurs particularitez de ce royaume: trois discours politiques sur les affaires du protecteur d'Angleterre, la reine de Suède, & du duc de Lorraine. Cologne: Chez Pierre Marteau, 1666
Stuart arms version 3. Stamped 'RELIE PAR SIMIER'

CALLCOTT, Maria, Lady
Three months passed in the mountains east of Rome, during the year 1819.
London: Longman, Hurst, Rees, Orme and Brown, 1820
Stuart arms, version 5. Label 'NEW/BOOK-BINDER/11, STRAND'

Fig. 96
Armorial 1, probably before 1812 (when Charles Stuart became a Knight of the Bath). This lacks any mark of cadency for him as a younger son

96

CARLETON, Dudley, Viscount Dorchester and Gaspard MONOD
Lettres, mémoires et négociations du chevalier Carleton, ambassadeur ordinaire de Jacques I, roi d'Angleterre, & c. aupres des Etats-Genéraux des Provinces-Unies: dans le tems de son ambassade en Hollande depuis le commencement de 1616 jusqu'à la fin de 1620. La Haye, Leiden: Chez Pierre Gosse, Junior [et] Elie Luzac, fils, 1759. 3 vols
Stuart arms version 2

CARTER, Elizabeth and Catherine TALBOT
A series of letters between Mrs Elizabeth Carter and Miss Catherine Talbot from the year 1714 to 1770, to which are added Letters from Mrs Elizabeth Carter to Mrs Vesey, between the years 1763 and 1787. London: F.C. and J. Rivington, 1809
Ink inscription 'Louisa Stuart'

CERVANTES, Saevedra Miguel de
Don Quixote de la Mancha. London: W. Stockdale, 1819. 4 vols

COLMAN, George
The dramatic works of George Colman the younger, with an original life of the author. Paris: Malpeyre, 1823-1824. vol. 2

DEPPING, Georges-Bernard
La Suisse: ou, Tableau historique, pittoresque et moral des cantons helvétiques' moeurs, usages costumes, curiosités naturelles, etc. Paris: A. Eymery, 1822. 4 vols

DODSLEY, Robert
A collection of poems in six volumes. London: Printed by J. Hughes for J. Dodsley, 1766
Stuart arms version 5

ELLIS, Henry, Sir
Original letters, illustrative of English history; including numerous royal letters; from autographs in the British Museum, and one or two other collections. London: Printed for Harding and Lepard, 1827. 4 vols
Stuart arms version 4

FAUCHE-BOREL, Louis
Mémoires de Fauche-Borel. Paris: Moutardier, 1829. 4 vols
Stuart arms version 4

GACON-DUFOUR, Marie Armande Jeanne
Mémoires, anecdotes secrètes, galantes, historiques et inédites sur mesdames de la

Vallière, de Montespan, de Fontanges, de Maintenon, et autres illustres personnages du siècle de Louis XIV. Paris: Chez Leopold Collin, 1807. 2 vols
Stuart arms version 3. Bookplate of F. Germain Lugd

GROSLEY, Pierre Jean
A tour to London, or New observations on England, and its inhabitants. London, printed for Lockyer Davis, 1772. 2 vols

GUARINI, Battista
Il pastor fido: tragi-commedia pastorale. Paris: Nella stamperia di Fr. Amb. Didot a spese di Gio. Cl. Molini, 1782. 2 vols
Stuart arms version 3

HAMILTON, Anthony, Count
Contes d'Hamilton. Paris: P. Didot, 1815
Stuart arms version 3

HEAD, Francis Bond, Sir
Rough notes taken during some rapid journeys across the Pampas and among the Andes. London: J. Murray, 1826
Stuart arms version 4

HEAD, George, Sir
Forest scenes and incidents, in the wilds of North America; being the diary of a winter's route from Halifax to the Canadas, and during four months' residence in the woods on the borders of Lakes Huron and Simcoe. London: J. Murray, 1829
Stuart arms version 4

HOMER
The Odyssey of Homer. London: Printed for Bernard Lintot, 1725-1726. 5 vols
Translation by Alexander Pope
Stuart arms version 5

JANIN, Jules Gabriel and Louis Eugene LAMI
The American in Paris during the summer being a companion to the 'Winter in Paris'; or 'Heath's picturesque annual for 1844'. London: Longman, Brown, Green and Longmans; Appleton and son, 1844
Ink inscription 'E.S. de R.'

JANIN, Jules Gabriel and Louis Eugene LAMI
The American in Paris, or, Heath's picturesque annual for 1843. London: Longman, Brown, Green and Longmans, 1843

Ink inscription 'E.S. de R.'
JONES, Stephen
A new biographical dictionary; containing a brief account of the lives and writings of the most eminent persons and remarkable characters in every age and nation. [London?]: Printed for G.G. and J. Robinson, 1796

JUNIUS
The letters of Junius. Paris: Malepeyre, 1822. vol. 2

Kalendario manual y guia del forasteros en Madrid para el año de 1798. Madrid: Imprenta Real de la Gazeta, 1798
Royal arms of Spain

LA COLONIE, Jean-Martin
Mémoires de Monsieur de La Colonie, marechal de camp des armées de l'électeur de Bavière ... Bruxelles: Aux depens de la Companie, [1737?]. vol. 2
Stuart arms version 2

LA FAYETTE, Madame de (Marie-Madeleine Pioche de la Vergne)
La princesse de Clèves; suivie de La princesse de Montpensier. Paris: P. Didot, 1815
Stuart arms version 3

LA FAYETTE, Madame de (Marie-Madeleine Pioche de la Vergne)
Zayde: histoire espagnole. Paris: P. Didot, 1815
Stuart arms version 3

LAIGUE, A.L. de
Les familles françaises considerées sous le rapport de leurs prérogatives honorifiques héréditaires, ou, Recherches historiques sur l'origine de la noblesse ... Paris: De l'Imprimerie Royale, 1818
Stuart arms 3

LALANDE, Joseph Jerome le Français de
Voyage d'un françois en Italie, fait dans les années 1765 & 1766. Contenant l'histoire & les anecdotes les plus singulieres de l'Italie, & sa description ... Yverdon, 1769-90. 8 vols

LAMOTHE-LANGON, Etienne Leon, baron de
Mémoires de Madame la comtesse Du Barri. Paris: Mame et Delaunay-Vallée, 1829-30. 6 vols

Stuart arms version 3
LANDON, Charles Paul
Annales du musée et de l'école moderne des beaux-arts. Receuil de gravures au trait, contenant la collection complète des peintures et sculptures de Musée Napoléon; et de celui de Versailles; les objets les plus curieux du Musée des monumens français; les principales productions des artistes vivans, en peintures, sculpture et architecture [edifices publics, etc.; avec des notices historiques et critiques]. Paris: C.P. Landon, 1807-1827. 7 vols
Stuart arms version 3

LECOMTE, Pierre Charles
Mémorial, ou Journal historique: impartial et anecdotique de la Révolution de France. Paris: Duponcet, 1801-1803. 3 vols
Stuart arms version 2

LEMAIRE DE BELGES, Jean
Le promptuaire des conciles de leglise catholique, auec les scismes & la differece diceul. [Lyons]: On les véd a Lyon, en la boutique de Romain Morín libraire, 1533. Printed by Denys de Harsy
Stuart arms version 2

LETI, Gregorio
Il putanismo do Roma, or, The history of the whores and whoredom of the popes, cardinals, and clergy of Rome: discovered by a conclave of ladies convened for the election of a new pope. Amsterdam, 1679
Stuart arms version 5

LETI, Gregorio
Vita di Sisto V, pontefice romano. Amsterdam: Per G.& E. Janssonio a Waesberge, 1693
Stuart arms version 1

LETI, Gregorio
Vita de Sisto V, pontefice romano. Amsterdam: Per Jassonio-Waesberge, 1721
Stuart arms version 1

LOMENIE, Louis-Henri, comte de Brienne and François BARRIERRE
Mémoires inédits de Louis-Henri de Loménie, comte de Brienne, secrétaire d'état sous Louis XIV. Paris: Ponthieu et Cie., 1828
Stuart arms version 4

97

Fig. 98
Armorial 3, probably 1815-28. This version is the most commonly found on the books in the Bequest

98

LOUVILLE, Charles Auguste d'Allonville, marquis de
Mémoires secrets sur l'établissement de la maison de Bourbon en Espagne. Paris: Maradan, 1818. 2 vols
Stuart arms version 3

MACKENZIE, Henry
The Mirror: a periodical paper, published at Edinburgh in the years 1779 and 1780. London: Printed for A. Strahan and T. Cadell and for W. Creech, Edinburgh, 1794. 3 vols

MACKINLAY, John
An account of Rothesay Castle. Greenock: Printed by William Scott, 1816
Stuart arms version 5

MARIVAUX, Pierre Carlet de Chamblain de
Le paysan parvenu, ou, Les mémoires de M***. Paris: Chez la veuve Duchesne, 1764. 3 vols
Stuart arms version 5

MONTAGU, Mary Wortley, Lady
The works of the Right Honourable Lady Mary Wortley Montagu: including her correspondence, poems and essays: published, by permission, from her genuine papers. London: R. Phillips, 1803. 5 vols
Stuart arms version 5

MONTAGU, Mary Wortley, Lady
The letters and works of Lady Mary Wortley Montagu. London: R. Bentley, 1837. 3 vols

NAUDRE, Philippe
Histoire abregée de la naissance & du progrez du kouakerisme: avec celle de ses dogmes. Cologne: Chez Pierre Marteau, 1692
Stuart arms version 2

PÖLLNITZ, Karl Ludwig, Freiherr von
Nouveaux mémoires du baron de Pollnitz, contenant l'histoire de sa vie et la relation de ses premiers voyages. Liège: Chez Joseph Demen, 1738. 2 vols
Stuart arms version 2

POPE, Alexander
The essay on man and other poems. Chiswick: From the press of C. Whittingham, 1822
Book plate of Beaumont Hotham

Fig. 99
Armorial 4, after 1828, an adaptation of version 3 with the coronet (for the barony) struck separately

Portraits des officiers et savans attachés a l'armée d'Egypte. [S.l., ca. 1796]
Stuart arms version 3

POTOCKI, Jan, Hrabia
Voyage dans les steps d'Astrakhan et du Caucase, histoire primitive des peuples qui ont habitée anciennement ces contrées, nouveau periple du Pont-Euxin. Paris: Merlin, 1829. 2 vols
Stuart arms version 4

RICCABONI, Marie Jeanne de Heurles Laboras de Mezieres
Histoire du marquis de Cressy; suivie d'Ernestine. Paris: P. Didot, 1815

RICCABONI, Marie Jeanne de Heurles Laboras de Mezieres
Lettres de mistriss Fanny Butlerd à mylord Charles Alfred, comte d'Erford. Paris: P. Didot, 1814
Stuart arms version 3

ROUSSEAU, Jean-Jacques
Julie, ou la nouvelle Héloise. Lettres de deux amans: habitans d'une petite ville au pied des Alpes. Amsterdam: Chez Marc Michel Rey, 1761. 6 vols

Stuart arms version 5
RUSTAING DE SAINT-JORY
Mémoires secrets de la cour de France, contenant les intrigues du cabinet, pendant la minorité de Louis XIV. Paris: Chez François Girardi, 1733
Stuart arms version 1

SHERIDAN, Richard Brinsley
The dramatic works of R. B. Sheridan: with an original life of the author. Paris: Malpeyre, 1822. vol. 3

TASSO, Torquato
La Gierusalemme liberata. Genoa: G. Bartoli, 1590

ULPIAN
De edendo. Göttingen: Apud Joannem Fridericum, 1809
Stuart arms version 3

VLIET, JAN van
Iani Vlitii Venatio novantiqua. [S.l.]: Ex officina Elzeviriana, 1643
Stuart arms version 2. Stamped 'RELIE PAR SIMIER'

WALPOLE, Horace
Letters of Horace Walpole, earl of Orford, to Sir Horace Mann, British envoy at the court of Tuscany. London: R. Bentley, 1833. vols 1 & 2
Armorial bookplate of Henry Frampton

WALPOLE, Horace
Letters of Horace Walpole, earl of Orford, to Sir Horace Mann; his Britannic Majesty's resident at the court of Florence, from 1760 to 1785. London: R. Bentley, 1843-44. 2 vols
Armorial bookplate of Henry Frampton

Other Books

ARNOUX, Alexandre
Romancero moresque. Paris: H. Piazza, 1921
Ink inscription to Bettine, Lady Abingdon

DUTTON, Ralph
The Victorian home: some aspects of nineteenth century taste and manners.

London: Batsford, 1954

FERGUSON, James
The art of drawing in perspective: made easy to those who have no previous knowledge of the mathematics. London: Printed for W. Strahan; and T. Cadell in the Strand, 1775
Pencil inscription 'T. Hole'

HAROLD, André-Ferdinand
Nala et Damayanti. Paris: H. Piazza, 1923. Card inscribed to Bettine, Lady Abingdon

HOLME, C. Geoffrey and Randall DAVIES
Caricature of today. London: The Studio, 1928

LAVER, James and Henry D. DAVRAY
XIXth century French posters. London: Nicholson and Watson, 1944

MASSINGHAM, Betty
Turn on the fountains: a life of Dean Hole. London: Gollancz, 1974

Fig. 100
Armorial 5, after 1828, his arms as Lord Stuart de Rothesay, the title granted to him in that year

PRESTON, Arthur Edwin and Agnes Charlotte BAKER
The Abingdon Corporation plate: some notes on the Abingdon plate and kindred treasures, and on the donors and the occasions of the gifts. Oxford: Printed at the University Press by C. Batey, 1958

ROYAL SOCIETY OF PORTRAIT PAINTERS
Catalogue of the sixty-ninth annual exhibition, at the Royal Institute Galleries ... November 21st to December 20th 1962 London: The Society, 1962

STUART WORTLEY, Violet
A prime minister and his son, from the correspondence of 3rd Earl of Bute and of Lt. General the Hon. Sir Charles Stuart, K.B. London: J. Murray, 1925

STUART WORTLEY, Violet
Highcliffe and the Stuarts. London: J. Murray, 1927

STUART, Charles, General
Short sketch of the life of Louisa Stuart, Marchioness of Waterford. London: Printed by Spottiswoode & Co., 1892

WHISTLER, Rex and Lawrence WHISTLER
Rex Whistler, 1905-1944: a memorial exhibition. London: The Arts Council, 1960

Manuscripts

Deed appointing Sir Charles Stuart as a Knight Companion of the Order of the Bath, dated 14 November 1812

Visitors' book for Highcliffe Castle, 1869-1926

Letter from William IV to the Duke of Orleans, thanking him for his condolences on the death of George IV, dated 14 July 1830

NOTE FOR PAGE 95
1. *Catalogue of the Valuable Library of the late Lord Stuart de Rothesay...to be sold... Thursday 31st May 1855 and fourteen following days.* The total of lots was 4323.

99

APPENDIX: STAINED GLASS

In 1989 the Museum acquired by purchase three further items from the collections at Highcliffe. Although these do not form part of the Bettine, Lady Abingdon Collection, they are of great importance and should be listed here. The high quality of much of the stained glass collected for Highcliffe has been mentioned in the essay on Lord Stuart de Rothesay's acquisitions (p. 37). Most of this remained *in situ* after the departure of the missionary order which owned Highcliffe following 1949. Its subject matter was, of course, particularly consonant with their use of the house, and indeed the hall became, for a while, a chapel. After 1967 fire and dereliction attacked the house. Some of the stained glass was removed to ensure its survival. Eventually three panels were purchased by the Museum. These are surviving fragments from the glass ordered for the Abbey of Saint-Denis, Paris, in the mid-12th century by Abbot Suger. It is not certain how Lord Stuart de Rothesay came by these panels.[1] There was an established trade in glass to England and English dealers were known, but judging by the extent of Lord Stuart de Rothesay's known purchases in France, it is likely that he

may have acquired the panels there and we should bear in mind the reference to 'wood, glass etc.' made by Gunn in a letter of 30 December 1832 (quoted on p. 34).

A.1
Panel from the Border of the *Infancy of Christ* Window
French, 1140-45, from the Abbey of Saint-Denis
Stained glass
L: 30.2cm W: 18.6cm
Accession no: C.63-1989

A.2
Part of a Roundel with Scene from the *Life of Saint Benedict* (The Saint Healing a Child)
French, 1140-45, from the Abbey of Saint-Denis
Stained glass
H: 58cm W: 29.3cm
Accession no: C.64-1989

Fig. 101
A.1 Panel from the border of the *Infancy of Christ* window, from the Abbey of Saint-Denis; French, 1140-45, re-set at Highcliffe Castle, 1830-40

Fig. 102
A.2 Part of a roundel with a scene from the *Life of St Benedict* (The Saint Healing a Child), from the Abbey of Saint-Denis; French, 1140-45

Fig. 103
A.3 Part of a roundel with a scene from the *Nativity* (The Shepherds Going to Bethlehem), from the Abbey of Saint-Denis; French, 1140-45

A.3
Part of a Roundel with Scene from the *Nativity* (the Shepherds going to Bethlehem)
French, 1140-45, from the Abbey of Saint-Denis
Stained glass
H: 56.7cm W: 29.3cm
Accession no: C.65-1989

NOTE FOR PAGE 100

1. Corpus Vitrearum Medii Aevi, France I: Louis Grodecki, *Les Vitraux de Saint-Denis* (Paris: Comité International d'Histoire de l'Art, 1976), p.68.

BIBLIOGRAPHY

This is not a comprehensive bibliography but a list of the works which were most widely used in the compilation of the handbook. Sources for information on particular items in the collection or for detailed points made in the text are given in full in notes.

Family History - Stuart de Rothesay

Franklin, Robert A., *Lord Stuart de Rothesay (1779-1845)* (Upton-upon-Severn: Images/Robert Franklin, 1993)

Hare, Augustus, *The Story of Two Noble Lives* (London: George Allen, 1893)

Harriet, Countess of Granville, *A Second Self*, ed. Virginia Surtees (Wilton, Wiltshire: Michael Russell, 1990)

Hole, Tahu, *Fragments from a Family Tapestry* (privately printed, 1972)

Stuart Wortley, Violet, *Highcliffe and the Stuarts* (London: John Murray, 1927)

Stuart Wortley, Violet, *Magic in the Distance* (London: Hutchinson, 1949)

Stuart Wortley, Violet, *Sophy, the Winkle Picker* (Christchurch: Christchurch Times, 1941)

Stuart Wortley, Violet, *Life Without Theory* (London: Hutchinson & Co., 1946)

Surtees, Virginia, *Charlotte Canning* (London: John Murray, 1975)

The papers of Lord Stuart de Rothesay are extensive, as might be expected for such an active diplomat. The National Register of Archives lists papers in the British Library, PRO, PRO of Northern Ireland, the National Library of Scotland (NLS), Edinburgh University Library, the Library of All Soul's College, Oxford, Durham University Library, Nottingham University Library, Buckinghamshire Record Office, the University of Minnesota Library, the University of Chicago Library, the Lilly Library and Indiana University Library. Most of these collections are not yet sorted and listed and it was not possible to search them for this study. The papers in the National Library of Scotland are, however, ordered, and provided much of the material used here, from personal letters scattered throughout Stuart's diplomatic correspondence.

Personal History - Mr and Mrs T.R.P. Hole

Miall, Leonard, *Inside the BBC* (London: Weidenfeld & Nicolson, 1994)

Highcliffe

Hussey, Christopher 'Highcliffe Castle', *Country Life*, XCI (1942), pp. 806-9; 854-7; 902-5

London, Leigh, Sotheby and John Wilkinson, *Catalogue of the Valuable Library of the late Lord Stuart de Rothesay ... to be sold ... Thursday 31st May 1855 and fourteen following days*

London, Christie Manson & Wood, *Catalogue of the Contents of Highcliffe Castle, Highcliffe, Hants., the property of The Rt. Hon. The Earl and Countess of Abingdon ... held on the premises, Tuesday, July 5th, 1949 and two following days*

London, Christie Manson & Wood, *Fine French and Continental Furniture, Objects of Art, Tapestries, Eastern Rugs and Carpets. Thursday 10 December 1987*

O'Donnell, Roderick, 'W J Donthorn (1799-1859): architecture with "great hardness and decision in the edges"', *Architectural History*, 21 (1978), pp. 83-92

Powell, J.H., 'Highcliffe Castle, near Christchurch, Hampshire', *Transactions of the Ancient Monument Society*, XXV (1967), pp. 82-94

Waterford, Louisa, Lady, 'Highcliffe in the Eighteen Thirties. Recollections up to the age of Twelve', *Highcliffe Parish Magazine*, June 1891, re-published by Highcliffe Parish Magazine, n.d (1950s)

Worsley, Giles 'Highcliffe Castle, Dorset', *Country Life*, CLXXIX (1986), pp. 1428-32

Carlton House Terrace

London County Council, *The Survey of London*, vol. XX, 'Trafalgar Square and Neighbourhood' (The Parish of St Martin-in-the-Fields, Part III) (1940)

Mansbridge, Michael, *John Nash* (Oxford: Phaidon, 1991)

Hôtel de Charôst

Beal, Mary, and John Cornforth, *British Embassy, Paris. The House and its Works of Art* (London: Government Art Collection, 1992)

Friedman, Joseph, *British Embassy - Paris: the history of a house 1725-1985*, 4 vols. Foreign and Commonwealth Office (1985), internal, unpublished FCO document

Friedman, Joseph, *Catalogue of the Bonaparte Borghese Collection of furniture and bronzes*, 2 vols. Foreign and Commonwealth Office (1985), internal, unpublished FCO document

Maréchal Ney / Hôtel de Saisseval

La Rue de Lille, Hôtel de Salm (Paris: Delegation a l'Action Artistique de la Ville de Paris, 1983)

Ministère d'Etat Chargé des Affaires Culturelles. Direction des Archives de France, *Les Archives du maréchal Ney et de sa famille conservées aux Archives nationales*. Inventaire par Simone de Saint-Exupéry et Chantal de Tourtier (Paris: Archives nationales, 1962)

Perrin, Eric, *Le Maréchal Ney* (Paris: Librairie Académique Perrin, 1993)

Collecting

Bellaigue, Geoffrey de, 'Edward Holmes Baldock' I and II, *Connoisseur*, CLXXXIX (1975), pp. 290-99, CXC (1975), pp. 18-25

Cornforth, John, 'French Genius in the Regency Taste', *Country Life*, CXXXIX (1966), pp. 650-52

Carlton House. The Past Glories of George IV's Palace. Exhibition, The Queen's Gallery, London (1991-2)

French Connections. Scotland and the Arts of France. Exhibition, Royal Scottish Museum, Edinburgh (1985)

Wainwright, Clive, *The Romantic Interior* (London: Yale U.P., 1989)

Furniture

Alcouffe, Daniel, Anne Dion-Tenenbaum, Pierre Ennès eds, *Un Age d'or des arts décoratifs 1814-48* (Paris: Réunion des musées nationaux, 1991)

Grandjean, Serge: *Empire Furniture* (London: Faber & Faber, 1966)

Kjellberg, Pierre, *Le Mobilier Français du XVIIIe Siècle* (Paris: Editions de l'Amateur, 1989)

Ledoux-Lebas, Denise: *Les Ebénistes du XIXe Siècle* (Paris: Les Editions de l'Amateur, 1989)

Lefuel, Hector, *Georges Jacob, Ebéniste du XVIIIe Siècle* (Paris: Editions Albert Morancé, 1923)

INDEX

Note: The index omits names of artists on pages 80-87 and authors of books on pages 95-99 where works are listed in alphabetical order.